Praise for
Third Base Ain't What It Used to Be

"What do kids need to know in order to grow up sexually safe and healthy? Few questions are more important (and more often asked) by parents. Logan Levkoff provides answers in a very readable and powerful book. She provides parents with facts, communication tips, and clear insight. She even challenges us to examine our own beliefs and values regarding sex. As both a professional and a parent, I highly recommend this book!"
—Michael Gurian, author of *The Wonder of Boys*
and *The Wonder of Girls*

"Sexuality is a whole new ball game for kids today. You'd think parents who came of age in the seventies and eighties would be sex-ed pros; the opposite is true! Moms and dads don't want to talk about IT. This book is a must-have for parents of girls and boys in our oversexed culture. Logan Levkoff delivers up-to-the-minute access to the way tweens and teens perceive sexual issues and strategies for parents to guide young people toward sexual knowledge, restraint, and fulfillment. She goes straight to the point in every chapter with invaluable 'questions teens want answers to.' Now parents will have those answers."
—Margaret Sagarese, coauthor of *The Roller-Coaster Years*
and *Boy Crazy!: Keeping Your Daughter's Feet on the
Ground When Her Head Is in the Clouds*

continued...

"Our children need to know the facts about their bodies, because their lives depend upon it. This is a well-written, easy-to-read, and easily understood book for parents, sex education teachers, and anyone who wants to better communicate with young people about sexuality. In an objective, nonthreatening manner, it will give you options when you wonder, 'Oh no, what do I say now?' You can read it straight through, then use it as a guide for communicating healthy sexuality from birth through adolescence. I highly recommend it to anyone who wishes to be a better parent."

—M. Joycelyn Elders, M.D.

third base ain't what it used to be

What Your Kids Are Learning
About Sex Today—
and How to Teach Them to Be
Sexually Healthy Adults

LOGAN LEVKOFF, M.S.

 New American Library

New American Library
Published by New American Library, a division of
Penguin Group (USA) Inc., 375 Hudson Street,
New York, New York 10014, USA
Penguin Group (Canada), 90 Eglinton Avenue East, Suite 700, Toronto,
Ontario M4P 2Y3, Canada (a division of Pearson Penguin Canada Inc.)
Penguin Books Ltd., 80 Strand, London WC2R 0RL, England
Penguin Ireland, 25 St. Stephen's Green, Dublin 2,
Ireland (a division of Penguin Books Ltd.)
Penguin Group (Australia), 250 Camberwell Road, Camberwell, Victoria 3124,
Australia (a division of Pearson Australia Group Pty. Ltd.)
Penguin Books India Pvt. Ltd., 11 Community Centre, Panchsheel Park,
New Delhi - 110 017, India
Penguin Group (NZ), 67 Apollo Drive, Rosedale, North Shore 0632,
New Zealand (a division of Pearson New Zealand Ltd.)
Penguin Books (South Africa) (Pty.) Ltd., 24 Sturdee Avenue,
Rosebank, Johannesburg 2196, South Africa

Penguin Books Ltd., Registered Offices:
80 Strand, London WC2R 0RL, England

First published by New American Library,
a division of Penguin Group (USA) Inc.

First Printing, October 2007
10 9 8 7 6 5 4 3 2 1

REGISTERED TRADEMARK—MARCA REGISTRADA

LIBRARY OF CONGRESS CATALOGING-IN-PUBLICATION DATA:

Levkoff, Logan.
Third base ain't what it used to be/Logan Levkoff.
    p. cm.
Includes bibliographical references.
ISBN: 978-0-451-22249-7
1. Sex instruction.   2. Communication in the family.   3. Parent and child.   I. Title.
HQ57.L47   2007
649'.65—dc22   2007012660

Set in New Caledonia with display in Base Nine
Designed by BTDNYC

Printed in the United States of America

This book is dedicated to my family—my parents, Susan and Steven Levkoff, for teaching me about tolerance and respect and giving me a model of what good parenting is all about; my husband, Louis Cortes, for over a decade of unconditional love, laughter, and counsel; my son, Maverick, for inspiring me to be a better person and allowing me to put my career to good use on a daily basis; and to my grandparents, Bea and Milton Shapiro, for everything.

Contents

third base ain't
    what it used to be

Introduction

"What is sex, anyway?"
I have asked this question of hundreds of children and teens over the years, and while there has never been a unanimous answer, attitudes toward sex have definitely changed. There is great debate over which sexual behaviors count and which don't. Many of my students have suggested, "Oral sex isn't sex. It's just third base." Even if you don't remember what the baseball analogy was when you were in school, the way children view sex is different now. And that's where I come in.

FROM PRESIDENT TO SEX EDUCATOR TO PARENT

Most children don't wake up one day and say, "When I grow up, I want to be a sex educator." I certainly didn't. I always thought that I was going to be the first female president of the United States. If that failed, I would consider a job as an attorney or Supreme Court justice. A career that had to do with sex was never part of my grand plan. But while my dreams of being in politics eventually waned, my desire to explore provocative subjects for a mass audience never faded. This desire to stimulate dialogue stemmed from my family— they ingrained in me both a sense of responsibility and a lot of confidence, a perfect combination for someone who talks about sex for a living.

If you think that my parents were liberal hippies who espoused ideals of free love, you would be very much mistaken. My own sexuality education was pretty minimal, from what I remember. My parents bought me a book called *Mommy, Where Do Babies Come From?*, in which two children's quest to discover how babies were made took them to a florist, where they learned about pollination, to a bird specialist, who taught them about bird fertilization, and then, finally, back home to the boy's mother to learn about human reproduction. Though the last few pages talked about the penis and vagina, they didn't offer any illustrations of the parts—only a watercolor drawing of a mommy sitting in a rocking chair while her son and his friend listened at her feet. In hindsight, the book was sweet, but not very informative.

It was the kids on the school bus who supplied the gory and graphic details of my sex education (many of which, as you can imagine, were barely accurate). But even though a lot of what the big bully in the backseat told us seemed crazy (like you could get pregnant if someone spit on you when they had an erection), we believed him. He became our expert.

So how did I get from the back of that school bus to the front of the classroom? In my quest to discover why I became a sexologist, I came across some interesting artifacts hiding in my parents' attic. My mom had requested that I go through some of my old things. I believe her exact words were "Keep it or trash it—just not here." In my search, I found my third-grade diary. As Spin the Bottle parties hadn't begun until I was in seventh grade, I didn't expect to find anything interesting.

"April 24, 1985. I stayed up late to watch *Dynasty*. Alexis and Dex were kissing with tongue. He grabbed her and her bra almost popped open. Then they started making—oops—having sex— Yeah! Ooh!" Okay, so if you have ever watched *Dynasty*, this is not surprising to you. Alexis Carrington bedded dozens of men, sometimes all in one episode. But I couldn't believe that my affinity for writing about sex may have started at age nine. I went through the rest of the diary and found at least twenty more descriptions of televised sexual escapades. Don't forget, television was much tamer then. I had probably managed to find most if not all the network sex there was at the time.

The truth is, despite my typically meager sexuality education, my proclivity toward sexual topics is actually in my blood. My late grandfather, who was my biggest supporter, never left his house without my business card in his pocket. (Whenever I spent time with my grandparents, there would always be a seventy-year-old friend asking me if I was "the granddaughter in the sex business." And then they would ask me their most personal sex questions. Believe me, if you thought seniors don't have sex, think again!) Though I never knew his mother, I felt connected to her, too. Lena, who I was named after, was a strong, liberated woman. In fact, she was one of the first women to go to the Margaret Sanger Center in New York City to get a pessary. (In today's language, that would be a diaphragm.)

Whether or not my career choice is related to my genetic makeup, I have learned that what most people shy away from, I am drawn to. I hope that my ability to speak honestly about sexuality encourages you to do the same thing in your homes, with the people you care most about. The umbrella of sexuality covers so much of who we are and what we believe in. And although I once dreamed of becoming president, now I can't imagine doing anything else.

I began my work in this field long before I had children of my own. But now, as a parent, I am doubly committed. I am terrified at the thought of those ignorant kids on the school bus as my son's sex educators. Today, it's not just the misinformation that seeps into our kids' brains, but the unspoken value system (or lack thereof) that seeps into our kids' lives and vocabulary. Our culture is full of mixed messages about sex. On the one hand we are puritanical—movies full of violence get lighter MPAA ratings than those with sex; on the other hand we are highly graphic, if not sexually exploitative—pop stars of all ages are portrayed as highly sexualized and some are even making and distributing their own personal sex tapes. Add to this mix our society's heavy proviolence stance and we have a real problem on our hands. If we don't challenge these views in our own homes, we default to them.

We are responsible for our children's sexuality education—for their values and their treatment of themselves and others. Whether we talk frequently or avoid the issue altogether, our participation, or lack thereof, sends a message. We teach even when we stay silent.

> My parents always laugh at me when I tell them that there are certain words that people cannot use around our son, Maverick. Not the words you're thinking of. Profanity is fine—it's the uglier, loaded terms with negative connotations that scare me. I teach children all the time who commonly call something or someone "faggy" instead of using the more palatable term "nerdy." No matter how old I get, the word "faggy" engenders so much frustration for me. By using the word—even if its context is completely innocent—we implicitly accept this "racial slur" when we should be challenging it. And let's be honest—the word doesn't just come from the school bus big mouth—it comes from all the kids, and it comes from us, their parents.

THE PHILOSOPHY OF THIS BOOK

As you will read in Chapter 2, sexuality educators construct their classes to be as "value-free" as possible. It is not our job to tell students what to believe (or what we personally do or don't do), but rather, we give them facts, tools, and multiple perspectives so that they can identify their own personal values. I believe that parents, however, should absolutely be teaching their children about their values, and their personal experiences. As parents you can be wonderful sexuality educators, because you can use your values and experiences to teach, but also because you engage with your children on a daily basis. In a classroom, I have limited time to work with my students; you have access to them every day. While they may not always follow your lead, your children will use your values to help them develop their own beliefs. Though I encourage you, as you read this book, to explore your own values regarding sexuality, mine are quite evident. For example, I believe in tolerance, healthy sexual communication, and the right to have sexual pleasure, both emotional and physical. The educational philosophy inherent in the book is also in line with the SIECUS (Sexuality Information and Education Council of the United States) *Guidelines for Comprehensive Sexuality Education* (2004). You will find that these ideas are expressed throughout the book, including, but not limited to:

- Sexuality is a natural and healthy part of living and all persons are sexual.
- Sexuality includes physical, ethical, social, spiritual, psychological, and emotional dimensions.
- Parents should be the primary sexuality educators of their children.
- Families provide children's first education about sexuality and share their values about sexuality with their children.
- In a pluralistic society, people should respect and accept the diversity of values and beliefs about sexuality that exist in a community.
- Sexual relationships should be reciprocal, based on respect, and should never be coercive or exploitative.
- Individuals, families, and society benefit when children are able to discuss sexuality with their parents and/or other trusted adults.
- Young people develop their values about sexuality as part of becoming adults.
- Young people explore their sexuality as a natural process of achieving sexual maturity.

• Young people who are involved in sexual relationships need access
  to information about health care services.

THAT BEING SAID . . .

When it comes to sex, most of us are clueless. Yes, we know how to
have sex, but we have no idea how to teach our kids about it. Even
if we purchase every parenting book there is, sex is a subject all its
own. For the most part, parenting books only skim the surface of
sexuality because we all come to parenting (and quite frankly, sex)
from different backgrounds and with a range of values. We are entitled to our values and shouldn't be afraid to share them with our
children—even if our kids don't agree. The purpose of this book
is to give you information so that you can impart both knowledge
and values to your kids. It is also a look into the sex-saturated world
that your kids are living in.

You are entitled to your own values about sexuality and you may
find that some of them are not in line with mine (which is perfectly
acceptable and not all that surprising). Yet we should be aware that
there is a clear difference between a value and a fact. It's one thing
to tell your children that you believe masturbation is a sin; it's quite
another to say, falsely, that masturbation will make you impotent
later in life. The same rule applies to the issue of sexual orientation.
Homosexuality is not a mental illness, even if you don't approve of
it. Trying to bolster your beliefs by resorting to myths and distor-
tions will only hurt your cause in the long run, when your kids find
out they're not true. Convey your values, *and* the facts, honestly.

Please keep in mind that this book is not intended to replace you or question your parenting skills. It was written to shed some light on the world that your kids are living in and simultaneously jog your own adolescent memories. It is arranged by topic, includes common questions that children and teens have asked me (in their own words), and offers tips and talking points for tackling these issues in your own home. My role in all of this is to be your guide, your peer (a fellow parent), and a professional. If after reading this you can manage to have at least one more conversation with your offspring about human sexuality, well, then I have done my job. Yours is about to continue.

Chapter One

BEFORE YOU CAN GET TO THE BIG TOPICS, YOU MUST BUILD THE FOUNDATION

SEX ED BEGINS AT BIRTH

If you have little kids, you are probably wondering why on earth you'd need a sex-ed book now. Well, sex education begins the second you bring your baby into the world. Everything you do and say matters. Even the environment you create sends implicit messages about gender roles to your newborn. If your son's room is decorated with planes, footballs, and guns, you are quietly teaching him about aggression. A soft frilly girl's room filled with dolls and kitchen sets conveys certain stereotypical roles to them as well. This doesn't mean that you need to turn tradition on its head, but it wouldn't be a bad idea to mix things up just a little bit. Giving dolls to our sons and cars to our daughters won't affect their sexual orientation later in life—it just gives them more options and lets them further explore their likes and dislikes.

Room decor aside, your use and choice of language is probably your child's first taste of sexuality education, and I have this pet (okay, more like a monster) peeve about using inaccurate terminology to describe your anatomy. Call me crazy, but I find slang terms offensive, particularly when they are coming out of the mouth of a toddler. I mean, honestly, do you really think it's less embarrassing for your little darling to ask, "Nana, do you have a wee-wee?" than "Nana, do you have a penis?"

I recognize that no one is perfect, not even my friends who know about my no-slang policy. My friend Sara invited me over to see her new daughter. When it came time to change her, Sara said, "Honey, Aunt Logan's never seen a baby giney before." I looked over at that beautiful girl and said, "Actually, Kate, your *vagina* is inside. Right now, Mommy's cleaning your *vulva*."

That's right—it's a vulva. And if we don't start teaching our kids what the real words are, they are bound to wind up as sexually screwed up as we are. Okay, so that's a little severe. But really, what's the harm in telling them the truth?

When I have my son on the changing table, I'll say, "Yes, sweetheart. That's your penis. Oh, yes, you have an erection. I know, isn't that great? And don't worry; there will be a time when Mommy isn't hovering over you when you have one." Don't we want our kids to know what's happening to their bodies? If you aren't sure of the answer, ask yourself this: Was there ever a time in your life when your ignorance about something sexual made you feel scared, embarrassed, or guilty? Is that something you'd wish on your own child?

As a parent, everything you say and do makes a difference. Every time you say, "Honey, do I look fat?" in front of your child, she gets a crash course in self-esteem and body-image politics. Every time you make a joke about someone looking or acting gay, even if you are the least homophobic person out there, your child gets a message about judging people. Yes, everything counts.

E ven if your kids are in diapers, they are still impressionable. If you are going to ask them, "Where are your eyes? Where are your feet? Where is your belly button?" don't forget to ask about their genitals. They need to know that their penis or vulva isn't invisible!

PLAYING DOCTOR, BATHING, AND OTHER TRICKY SITUATIONS

When it comes to touching, babies and toddlers are experts in exploring their bodies and others'. What better way for them to learn about themselves? If you have a kid at home, you better get over your squeamishness! Young children love to be naked and both boys and girls will fondle their genitals out of pure curiosity and giggles, and not because they are deliberately trying to be sexual. They will rub up against toys, bedposts, anything that creates a "good feeling." Your naked body, too, will be a place of great interest, and this goes beyond breast-feeding. From your breasts and vulva to your penis and testicles, your children will want to touch, grab, and grope. Sometimes they will ask for permission, and other times they will take what they want. There is absolutely nothing wrong with letting them touch you—as long as you are not uncomfortable. If they are looking at or touching you, teach them the names of your parts just as you teach them about theirs. As for being naked, no harm will come from your children looking at your naked body.

Naturally, families have different rules about nudity; some are quite free and others are more buttoned up, literally. If you're not comfortable being naked around your children, then don't be! But if you are, know that that's okay, too. Whatever you decide, the only thing that all children need to know is that their own bodies are off-limits to certain people. You are going to need to explain that there are some people who can touch their genitals—for example, at an examination at the doctor's office—and some who cannot. That being said, a toddler who is mesmerized by naked bodies is just that, a toddler.

Now, there will come a time when you catch your post-toddler child and his friend half naked or fully naked in an effort to learn about each other's bodies. "Playing doctor" is a natural activity that exemplifies our children's innate curiosity rather than a deep-seated depravity. If you find that this is going on, ask your child why they were playing, what they are curious about, and what, if anything, they learned. Though there is nothing wrong with a little consensual role-playing, some parents may respond quite negatively to this scenario. If that's the case, explain to your child that though she didn't do anything bad, some parents are not comfortable with nudity.

It is important to keep in mind that sexuality education during toddlerhood and early childhood is less about sex and more about allowing our children to see the world through their innocent eyes. For example, a mom came to me about her two boys, ages four and seven, who had started to touch each other's penises when they bathed together. They realized that by doing this they would get erections, which they called "getting strong." This had been going on for months without her worrying about it, but one night her husband saw it and became incensed. "That's it," he told his wife. "No more baths together." She wanted to know if she had done something terrible.

As with playing doctor, panic is a very common first response to this kind of scenario. But take a breath, parents. Even though these boys were touching each other, it wasn't consciously sexual. They just thought it was cool that their penises could "stand up and be strong." The last thing you want to do is to make your children feel guilty or ashamed about something perfectly innocent. We shouldn't color their experience with our own issues. If you're uncomfortable with their behavior, there are ways to stop mutual bathing without scarring your children emotionally. One way is simply to say, "You are getting too big to fit into the tub," or that you're afraid they do too much playing and not enough washing when they're in the tub. A direct approach, such as "I don't want you touching each other's penises," may backfire, because your children are going to ask you why, especially if they don't see their behavior as sexual. Of course, if your kids bathing together isn't an issue for you, that's fine, too. At the end of the day, you need to parent by your own rules. The key is doing so without making your children feel bad about something they don't understand.

What about kids bathing or showering with parents? There is no evidence that it causes any harm to a child, as long as the parent feels comfortable. Five-year-old Marni usually took showers with her mother, but one day she asked if she could shower with her father. Both parents said yes, but at the last minute decided the father should wear a bathing suit. You can imagine what happened; Marni spent the entire time asking why her father was sporting a bathing suit in the shower. In hindsight, her father realized he might have felt less awkward taking a shower the "regular way."

There is no right or wrong answer to this situation—you have to do what you are comfortable with. I don't think that being naked would have been a big deal. In fact, it would have provided Marni's parents an opportunity to talk to their daughter about the differences between men and women. I am afraid that by covering up, we inadvertently send the message that there is something wrong (and something bad) about our bodies and that we should be ashamed of them. You know your children and yourselves best, however, and as long as you are prepared to talk them through their questions, how you choose to parent is up to you.

There are also situations that emerge that parents find almost impossible to handle calmly—including what to do when your child (or God forbid, teen) walks in on you and your partner or spouse having sex. It will happen; it almost always does. But how you respond has a great deal to do with whether your child winds up in therapy later on in life (I'm totally kidding). If you should find yourselves in the throes of passion and your child shows up in your doorway, ask them first if everything is okay and then tell them that you are sharing some private time and that you will see them later. If it is later, and you feel the need to explain what you were doing, this is the time to talk about how people express love in many ways and that you were sharing a private moment with your partner, emphasis on "private." Teens will probably be freaked out entirely, but that's okay. They need to know that adults can have active and fulfilling sex lives no matter how old they are.

SO WHAT IF YOU DON'T WANT TO TALK TO THEM?

The harsh reality is that if we choose to ignore our kids' questions and concerns, especially those about sexuality, we're sending the message that they are not worthy of the information. Once kids believe that they are less worthy, they make unhealthy and uninformed decisions. By not supplying our youth with accurate information, we unintentionally send them off into the world unprepared and at risk. And that's when the media, and the kids on the school bus, take over and become their primary sexuality educators.

The bottom line is that sticking your head in the sand when it comes to discussing sex doesn't cut it. Even if you think *you* turned out fine without a parental heart-to-heart, realize that in the twenty-first century sexuality has new meanings and new implications. Even if we consider ourselves "cool parents," there are trends in childhood and adolescent sexuality that may be beyond our comprehension or experience. Back when we were in high school, the girls who had oral sex were called sluts, if we even found out that anyone was actually having it. Today, girls and boys are having it, and the old label may not apply. When we grew up, MTV showed music videos; now it shows raunchy dating games. Today, music is filled with sexually explicit lyrics, popular dances simulate sex, our celebrities are photographed without underwear, and billboards frequently show models without any clothes on, even if they are advertisements for a fashion house. We cannot deny that society is much more explicit now, and wherever you live, sexual imagery is omnipresent. If you haven't yet begun to talk to your kids about sex, I can assure you, your television has. Though this is alarming, it's never too late to make a difference.

Though some kids would rather run naked through their school than bring up sex with you, children of all ages are full of questions about sex. I know this firsthand, as I have had the privilege of working with hundreds of kids and teens each year discussing issues pertaining to human sexuality. What comes up first is confusion about the concept of sexuality—and what makes it different from "sex." Though it is commonly tossed around, "sexuality" is something we are all consumed with but really have no idea what it's all about. By defining sexuality—and understanding that it is more than just who we are attracted to—parents can begin to present a holistic picture of sex to their children. After I gave a lengthy explanation of sexuality, a child recently said to me, "Sex is what you do, sexuality is who you are." She couldn't have been more correct. Sexuality encompasses far more than how you have sex, or if you have it at all. Sexuality is a central part of our identity, and includes our feelings about our gender, how we express ourselves, our sexual orientation, our body image, and, yes, our sexual behaviors.

Tips for Talking

In almost every one of my classes, someone asks me, "How come you aren't embarrassed talking about s-e-x?" Maybe you've been wondering, too. I guess it's because I believe so strongly that the more comfortable we become talking about sexuality, the better we will treat ourselves and the sooner we will begin to make better decisions regarding our sexual choices.

I know that's what you want for your kids: for them to have the self-confidence and self-esteem to make good choices that will keep them safe and healthy. Sure, talking to your kids about these issues is scary. But it is so, so worth whatever slight discomfort you may feel. I always have my students collaborate on "group guidelines" to make our class discussion more comfortable. The following is a set of guidelines for you that may make these conversations less stressful.

1. **TAKE A DEEP BREATH.** It is perfectly normal to feel anxious or nervous. Just know that you are not the first person to have to do this, nor will you be the last. Instead of ducking a question that makes you nervous or tongue-tied, practice saying, "Even though this may be difficult for me to answer, I will do the best I can."

2. **MAKE IT SIMPLE.** Don't feel obligated to provide every last scrap of knowledge you possess. Make sure that you understand exactly what your child is asking and answer it. Then stop! For example, my mentor in graduate school used to tell the story of a little boy who came home and asked his mother, "Where do I come from?" The flustered mother racked her brain to come up with the appropriate answer. Finally she spilled her guts and told the boy about sexual intercourse, sperm, eggs, and the birthing process. The child looked up at her and shook his head. "Mommy, Joey comes from New York. Where do I come from?" Before answering a question, find out what your child knows and what specifically she is trying to find out. Keep it simple.

3. **NO CLUE? NO PROBLEM.** It's okay if you don't know the answer to a question. It's impossible to be an expert on all subjects. Let your child know this. Instead of covering up or getting upset, say, "Let's try to find the answer together." If it isn't appropriate that you make this a joint effort, assure your child that the question was a good one and that you will find the answer for him. Never let your children believe that their questions are bad or stupid!

4. **TIMING IS ESSENTIAL.** Sometimes a question is asked in an inappropriate setting or at an inappropriate time. It's perfectly reasonable not to answer, but assure your child that you will talk about it at another time. (Of course, this means that you need to follow through.) Timing is also important to kids. Some children tell me, "I wish my parents wouldn't talk about sex in front of my siblings. That's embarrassing!" You know, those children have a point. For them, the dinner table may not be the best place to get them to talk to you. It's your job as a parent to come up with a more comfortable, and convenient, learning environment.

5. **BE PATIENT.** Children ask lots of questions and may ask the same thing over and over again. Instead of becoming frustrated or angry, give the answer as many times as necessary. Sometimes a repeated question is a sign that a child is confused.

6. **PRACTICE MAKES ALMOST-PERFECT.** There's no such thing as the perfect conversation. No person can possibly conduct these kinds of conversations without any glitch . . . and you know what? That's okay.

7. **ACTIONS SPEAK LOUDER THAN WORDS . . . SOMETIMES.** What you don't say sends as many messages to your kids as what actually comes out of your mouth. So does your body language. If you are physically uncomfortable, your kids will see this and know

that they have found a way to push your buttons. If you get up from the table, look away, or nudge your partner every time your child brings up a question or makes a comment about sex, you can be assured that the same question will be asked at your next family gathering, if not in front of your boss.

8. **DON'T MAKE ASSUMPTIONS!** No matter how young or old your kids are, they are going to have questions about sex—all types of sex. Just because they ask doesn't mean that they are doing—or have any interest in doing—what they inquired about. It's just a question. If you jump to conclusions and start freaking out or lecturing, they'll never come to you for information or advice again.

Remember: Take advantage of all the opportunities available to talk to your children about sexuality. Share your beliefs and values in a nonthreatening way. If a sexual issue is in the news, on TV, or in a movie, use it as a springboard for discussing that issue with your child. Ask your child for his or her opinion—it will be a good litmus test of their values.

USE YOUR EXPERIENCES

A parent once said to me, "My daughter isn't going to listen to me. She thinks that I grew up one hundred years ago and don't know what her world is like." Well, you know what? It doesn't really matter. As a parent, you are entitled to speak your mind. And there is absolutely no harm in telling your kids how life was for you. There is no better way for kids to understand their parents than to hear about their lives—especially the parts we rarely talk about. So when you ask them what *their* world is like, they won't be able to use "You just don't understand" as an excuse.

AND NOW A MESSAGE FROM YOUR CHILDREN

I have told many of the groups I work with about this book and I've said, "I have an opportunity to tell parents a little something about your lives. What would you like them to know about you?" No matter how old they are, they love to answer this question. It is a safe way of telling you what they want, without getting grounded. So here goes. . . .

The young ones (ages nine to twelve) would rather you talk to them about sex at a time that's comfortable and not just convenient. They don't like to talk in front of their siblings, who make fun of them. They may not want to talk about something they saw in a movie immediately afterward, but would rather wait until they've had a chance to think about it. They may not want you to ask questions about their sex education class the minute they get home from school. And they definitely don't want to overhear you telling their grandmother about how their bodies are developing. What they would like is for you to ask *them* when a good time is, so that they can feel a little more at ease.

They also would prefer that you didn't tell them everything all at once. A little information at a time seems to work best with children, as they are not ready to hear all of the intricacies of sexuality in one sitting. (And to be honest, parents are often not able or prepared to do it all and do it well, at least not all at once.)

Teens' biggest gripe about how their parents handle the whole "sex thing"? Assuming that they are having sex just because you read something in a magazine or heard a story on the news. In recent years, the media has sensationalized teen sexuality in bold ways—for example, discussing a "phenomenon" called rainbow parties, where teenage girls put on different colors of lipstick and perform oral sex on boys, leaving a "rainbow" trail. I have asked many groups about whether they have participated in rainbow parties. Only a few students had heard about them, and that was because they had read about them in an article. The rest of the students were adamant that they didn't participate in these parties and hadn't heard of anyone who did. And they said they would be furious if their parents heard about this and assumed that of course their children were into it as well.

Your teens would also like you to know that saying "Don't have sex" is neither a sufficient nor effective statement. They already know you feel this way; what they want is for you to give them the tools to decide for themselves when the right time comes, whether it's tomorrow or years from now. And then there are the teens who say that "parents need to give it up"; they are eventually going to have sex, and you need to deal with it. You don't need to endorse it, but they would like you to be realistic.

Last, they really do want to know how their parents feel about sex. Teenagers make a lot of assumptions, including, "I bet my parents want me to be a virgin forever." But is that really what you want? This is the time to talk to them, when you can help them to structure their values appropriately and not just out of parental spite. We really do have an influence over our teenagers; we should use this to our advantage while they still need us.

ON BEING AGE-APPROPRIATE

Parents are anxious about what to tell and when to tell it. But children are far more capable of processing sexual information than we typically might believe. The subjects of anatomy, what actually happens during puberty, and how a baby is "made" should definitely be covered by the time a child reaches puberty. The chronology and depth of the other conversations don't need to be set in stone. Some young children may be ready to talk about sexual intercourse and some preteens may not. Your children can take the lead and give you a sense of what they need to know at a particular time. If your children are less inclined to speak to you, then you need to take a more active role. As long as you are flexible, your children will benefit.

Chapter Two

SEX AND VALUES: THE TOUGH QUESTIONS ARE STILL TOUGH . . . AND MAY BE GETTING EVEN TOUGHER

It is rare that any of my parent meetings become heated, but it has happened. Once I was explaining to a group of fourth-graders' parents what I would be teaching their children. My fourth-grade curriculum tends to be fairly tame. We were covering the basics of anatomy and puberty—nothing very provocative. Granted, issues of sexual orientation and sexual health do come up frequently, but not at my prompting. Inevitably, it's a child, not me, who brings up a sophisticated sexual question. Not that this is a big surprise—they are exposed to the same bombardment of sexual imagery that we are. They have questions and desperately need help processing what they see and hear.

As I described our program to thirty or so parents, one man in the back was visibly agitated. He was shifting in his chair and clenching his jaw. Finally he raised his hand and said, "I don't want you giving *my* daughter *your* values." When you are in the world of sexuality education, adversity doesn't come as a shock to you. I said, "You are certainly welcome to remove your daughter from our program, but please keep in mind that I don't teach according to my values. I present both sides of an issue and encourage your child to go home and talk to *you* about *your* values."

I added that puberty has very little to do with values. Physical development is a given, not a choice. Needless to say, this man was still annoyed, but he sat back in his chair while his wife rolled her eyes next to him. I have to say, I wasn't upset by his outburst. The fact is, it is almost impossible to talk about sex without discussing your values. As educators, we have to be particularly careful not to espouse our own values in a classroom—especially if our students are young and impressionable. But as parents, we have the power and privilege to tell it all as we see fit.

In case you were wondering, the angry father's daughter did attend my class and wound up asking me one of the most difficult questions I have ever had to answer: "How do you know if your father is cheating on your mother?" My heart sank—not because I didn't have an answer, but at the thought of a little girl being so intimately involved in her parents' troubled relationship. It's funny what we consider difficult questions. I can handle questions about abortion, gay marriage, and sex change operations, but parental infidelity makes me sweat.

Teachers, at least the ones who don't teach sexuality education, can be just as uncomfortable as parents when it comes to students' queries about sex. During the last few weeks of the 2004 presidential race, my class of eleven- and twelve-year-olds was chomping at the bit to talk about the most provocative elements of the debates. On one day, they wanted to talk abortion and gay marriage.

Though abortion wasn't in the curriculum, I never want to discourage anyone's questions. So I explained the definition of abortion and that there were two sides to the debate: One side believed that life began at conception; the other believed that life didn't begin until much later on in a pregnancy or at birth. And, of course, I told them that this was a perfect topic to talk about at home, because their parents could tell them what side of the debate they were on. It wasn't a heated argument by any means. The kids were great, telling each other how they felt and what they believed based upon the little information I had given them. What was most rewarding for me was that they felt comfortable asking these questions. The environment was "safe" enough that they didn't fear getting into trouble for asking about something as difficult as abortion, probably because they didn't even realize the political and personal implications of asking about it to begin with.

> It's okay for your children to question your values. They are trying to form their own identities and value systems. Let them explore both sides of an issue in a "hypothetical" way.

The next day a teacher confronted me about my class (as she'd heard it) "on abortion." I told her the truth. "Actually, one of the students asked a question and I answered it as simply as possible. It really wasn't a class on abortion. It was just a discussion."

Within seconds she began to rant and rave about how inappropriate it was to talk about abortion in class. I reminded her that abortion was a headline that week—and that children aren't oblivious. They had questions and it was better to give them accurate information than to let them pick it up on the streets.

At our next class, some kids told me that teacher had yelled at them for talking about sexuality in the hall. Though I hated that she scolded the children for doing what I encourage them to do—ask difficult questions—it gave us an opportunity to discuss why some people have a hard time talking about sexuality. The students were really surprised that an adult was incapable of talking about sex. Aren't adults supposed to be able to handle everything? They didn't get it.

Try explaining to children that adults are not always comfortable with the topic of sex. It was especially difficult in this case because the kids had finally developed the comfort and confidence to talk about sexuality without going into hysterics. If anything, the steadfast belief in the "perfection" of parents gives all of us an incentive to be better educators, because our children want us to be. Their world is shaped by us and they believe that their parents hold the key to all sorts of information, not just sex. And again, what happens if we are unwilling to talk to them? We implicitly let other sources, far less reputable and accurate sources, become the teachers.

Next time you and your spouse or partner have some time, ask each other some of these tough questions so that you can practice answering them. This also allows you to be on the same page as your parenting partner.

"WHEN IS IT OKAY TO GO OUT ON DATES?"

Eventually everyone has to answer this question. Kids and teens are curious about dating—what it means, when is the right time, and what dating entailed when you were growing up. Needless to say, dating has changed. Unless you demand it, your child's date may not come to your door and introduce him- or herself to you (though it is perfectly acceptable and recommended that you do demand this). Teens are dating online and meeting people who may or may not be what they appear to be on the computer screen. Teens are group dating—going out in packs where there is not necessarily a one-on-one encounter. And of course with the advent of cell phones and other technology, it is possible for parents to be in touch with their children at any and all times. Depending on your child's definition of "dating," you should take the time to determine what constitutes the "right time" for dating. And it is your right as a parent to set the rules as you see fit—but you should always have a reason for doing so, as your children won't simply accept at face value an arbitrary rule. You can share your concerns, your rules, and your own dating experiences in an effort to get them ready to date safely, however you choose to define that. But you should also allow your children to prove themselves to you, too. If they are responsible, give them enough credit to allow them some freedom, without you feeling like you have to let go completely.

"WHEN DID YOU HAVE SEX?"

Though value-rich subjects like abortion and sexual orientation can cause lots of parents concern, almost everyone dreads the more personal questions—the ones about their own sexuality and/or sex lives. These will come up, and you'll have a split second to decide how you want to proceed, so it is important to think beforehand about our answers and the messages we want to send to our kids. Don't overlook the option of delaying the inevitable; you can always say, "I really want to answer you, but I just need to think about this for a moment." This should buy you some time . . . but only a little.

> Don't jump to conclusions. Children who ask you about the right time to have sex aren't necessarily actively considering it. They are just trying to put many mixed messages about sex into perspective. And the fact that they are asking you is a good thing. They want *your* advice.

Some parenting guides suggest you don't have to share personal issues with your children. I disagree, for several reasons. First, our experiences give us a unique perspective—and give our children a unique look inside our lives. It can also be empowering for them; you trust them enough to be straightforward. Most important, it provides you with the perfect launchpad to explain why you have certain feelings about the things that they (or their "friends") are experimenting with. At the end of the day, it's up to you to decide how you want to tackle these complicated questions. But I have always found that it is best to be honest with your children. That doesn't mean you need to spill every deep dark secret you have, but you can certainly give your children a sense of where you come from.

My son is too young to interrogate me about my sex life, but believe me, I have been asked my share of embarrassing and uncomfortable questions. Within the first five minutes of a fifth-grade class, a student asked, "Have you had sex?" Here's my little secret: The key to answering these personal questions—especially when they are asked by children other than your own—is not answering them. It's not as easy as it sounds. The trick is to make the child believe you've answered it. For example, the situation I found myself in sounded a bit like this:

> **STUDENT:** "Have you had sex?"
>
> **ME:** "That's a great question. But I'm not sure if I can answer it. Does anyone know why?"
>
> **STUDENT:** "It's too personal?"
>
> **ME:** "Well, it is a personal question, but let's talk about it for a minute. What would you say if I told you that I have never had sex?"
>
> **STUDENT:** "We would think that you are lying. You are an adult."
>
> **ME:** "And what if I told you that I have had sex?"
>
> **STUDENT:** "Well, then it wouldn't be a big deal. You're an adult."
>
> **ME:** "So I guess it doesn't really matter then. Whether I say yes or no, you'll think I've had sex and it's no big deal because I'm an adult, right?"
>
> **STUDENT:** "Right."

The next time your child asks you a personal question, try having them explore how they would respond to possible answers. It takes some of the onus off of you to have to tell them, and it gives them an opportunity to think about what they are really asking. So if you can't (or don't want to) answer, throw it back at them.

Another technique is to answer the question they didn't ask. Say your child asks, "When did you have sex for the first time?" You can certainly tell her, if you choose, but how about explaining what went into your decision first? Why did you decide to have sex? What kind of relationship were you in? Were you responsible about protection? Were you happy with your decision? By the time you finish talking about the decision-making process, they may not even be interested in the original question anymore. In fact, you will have given your teen (this question about sexual decision making rarely comes from the twelve-and-under set) much more valuable information than whether you were sixteen or twenty-six when you lost your virginity.

Sometimes honesty is truly the only option, especially when you're struggling to establish a bond of trust. One of my first teaching opportunities was at a maternity residence in Manhattan. My students were pregnant girls aged twelve to seventeen who had been forced out of their foster homes. And for ten weeks I was responsible for talking to them about sex. If you are like them, you're wondering what on earth I was going to teach them that they didn't know already. Turns out, they didn't know a hell of a lot about sex, even though they had had it many times. After getting to know my students—and more important, after getting them to trust me— they turned the tables on me.

"Logan, is abstinence what *you* practice?"

After all the work it took to get them to trust me, this was a serious test. Seeing as they were all pregnant, some for the second time, I knew that abstinence was probably not a realistic option for them, so in my head I shaped what I thought was the best and most appropriate answer.

"At the moment, abstinence is not an option for me. I have been with the same man for five years, we are monogamous, we have been tested, and we practice safer sex." Now some of you may disapprove of my honesty, but that's what they needed. And I can assure you, if I had said, "Yes, I am abstinent," they would never have listened to another word I said.

Whatever the situation, there is nothing wrong with telling the truth as long as you are comfortable with it. You can share in increments or all at once. How you share isn't as important as the fact that you care enough to talk to your kids at all.

What messages do you want your children to receive about sex? If you take the time to think about these in advance, you will be able to craft your answers more effectively.

The 10 Most Common Questions About Values Children and Teens Want Answers To

1. WHEN DID YOU "DO IT"?

Hopefully we covered this one . . . but be prepared—they'll ask.

2. WHEN IS A GOOD TIME TO HAVE SEX?

There is no single "good time" to have sex. A person should be ready, emotionally and physically, before engaging in sexual intercourse. It is "bad" to have sex at any age when you're not ready. Readiness is measured by your emotions, your knowledge of the positive and negative outcomes of sexual intercourse, and your readiness to communicate with your partner about safer sex and its responsibilities.

3. IS IT OKAY TO HAVE SEX BEFORE MARRIAGE?

Instead of giving you my answer, I recommend that you think carefully about what messages you would like to impart to your children and go from there. If you believe that sex before marriage is okay, give them the qualities and criteria that you think make premarital sex appropriate. If you do not agree with premarital sex, back up your statement with the reasons why. In addition to giving your own view on premarital sex, you can throw the question back at your child. Use these value-based questions to learn what your child is thinking and what is shaping his or her values. This type of indirect assessment will give you an indication of what your child may need to know in the near future.

4. IS IT OKAY FOR PEOPLE TO LIVE TOGETHER BEFORE THEY GET MARRIED?

What was commonly called "living in sin" is now simply "cohabitation." Regardless of what name it goes by, many people have strong opinions about it. What did you do in your own life? Your experiences, and whether they were positive or negative, can help you construct your answer. But your teens have probably heard the old adage "Why buy the cow when you can get the milk for free?" You can use this question to discuss, challenge, or support cohabitation as well as use it as a means of talking to your children about how dating rituals have changed.

5. **DO YOU THINK IT IS OKAY FOR TEENAGERS TO HAVE SEX?**

   How do you possibly explain this? Let me try to help. You don't
   want to lie, but at the same time you want to assure your children
   that sex is not for the young—at least not for the very young.
   Perhaps the easiest way to tackle the issue of teen or premarital sex
   is to tell them that sex is an adult decision that is not always made
   by adults. Sex can be a wonderful experience between two people
   who love each other, but it comes with many responsibilities that
   young people aren't always ready to handle. And from here, it is
   quite easy to move on to what those responsibilities are. There is
   also a good chance that your kids will ask you if you think that it
   is okay for younger people to have sex, too.

6. **HOW FAR IS TOO FAR AT MY AGE?**

   When I was in seventh grade, I remember my mom telling me that it
   was okay to kiss, but that I shouldn't be doing anything else. The
   conversation sticks out in my mind because she so clearly conveyed
   her personal values to me. No matter how old your child is, she is
   wondering what type of experimentation is appropriate for her. Think
   back to when you were her age. What were you doing? Were you
   proud of your choices? If so, you can share your decisions with your
   child. If not, tell her what would have made your decisions better.

7. **HOW DO YOU FEEL ABOUT ABORTION?**

   I'm not going to tell you how your children and teens should feel
   about abortion. This is an issue that you need to clearly define for
   yourself and then explain to your child. I firmly believe that parents
   should be forthcoming and honest, and explain both sides to the
   abortion debate. This will help teens solidify their personal values
   regarding abortion.

8. WOULD YOU LET ME GO ON THE BIRTH CONTROL PILL?

Before you pass out, remember that your child may be asking this out of curiosity, not because she actually needs contraceptives. If she does in fact want a prescription, at least pat yourself on the back that she came to you for help. Even if it's a struggle, try to be calm. Keep in mind that there are states where minors can get contraceptives, abortion services, and family planning counseling without parental consent, so if your child is asking you, try to be as supportive as possible. (For a listing of countries and states and their laws on contraceptives, check out www.avert.org/aofconsent. htm.) In addition to or instead of giving a yes or no answer, try to explore her reasons for wanting to go on the pill, and use this as an opportunity to talk about the pros and cons of oral contraceptives.

9. DO YOU THINK THAT IT IS OKAY TO TAKE EMERGENCY CONTRACEPTION?

Emergency contraception (EC) is a high dose of hormones that a woman takes within seventy-two hours after having unprotected sex. It prevents pregnancy, but it doesn't protect against sexually transmitted diseases. It is most effective when the initial dose is taken within the first twenty-four hours after unprotected sex. If you have a teenager, arm yourself with the facts of EC so you're prepared to give an opinion about whether it's "okay" to take. Regardless of what you decide, a teen who asks about emergency contraception should be reminded that protection against both STDs and pregnancy should be their priority and that they should be using a condom whenever they decide to be sexually active.

10. WOULD YOU BE UPSET IF I HAD AN STD?

Your teen is trying to determine whether she can come to you for guidance if she has a sex-related health crisis. If you tell her that you would be angry, chances are she will go elsewhere (or nowhere) when she needs help. If your answer leads to your child confiding in you about an STD, do your best not to freak out. There is plenty of time for being judgmental—though that rarely works. Right now your teen needs to seek immediate treatment and inform any sexual partners so that they can be tested as well. She also needs a reeducation about safer sex and protection, but it should be done in a way that doesn't make her feel ashamed.

Chapter Three

ANATOMY AND PUBERTY

"I want to be just like Samantha on *Sex and the City*." If you were to hear this from a twentysomething, you might think: "Okay, she's sexually empowered, wants a high-profile career, and has fabulous friends. It could be worse." But this was not my reaction— this statement was coming from one of my twelve-year-old students.

You probably are wondering, "What is this girl doing watching *Sex and the City*? Where are her parents?" I wondered that, too, and thought about how dramatically life has changed since I first learned about sex.

When I was seven, my parents attempted to explain the birds and the bees to me with a book. It was large, lobster-red, and had a water-color picture of a mother and baby on the cover. The watercolors of flowers and people continued throughout the pages. But there were no penises, no vulvas, no significant illustrations whatsoever. It was more about baby making in the context of love. Love begat a child. Seed to egg to . . . well, kid.

Like most children, the bulk of my sex education came from the sixth-graders at the back of my elementary-school bus. There I learned terms like "fuck" and "jerk off." Today, the bus echoes with words like "vibrator," "threesome," and "blow job." While as a child I couldn't have told you what *any* of these words meant, I loved using these new terms with my friend Adam. We sat next to each other on the bus home and practiced saying these cool words out loud—but not loud enough so that anyone else could hear them.

If this sounds funny and—admit it—similar to your own experience, consider how surprised my father was when I threw one of these new phrases in his direction. After one too many admonitions to "clean your room," I said, "Oh, Dad, jerk off!" Since I was quickly sent to my room, I had a feeling that "jerk off" was not a term I should have used with my father. But I didn't really get it. If someone was annoying and being a jerk, "jerk off" seemed like a clever way of saying, "Leave me alone."

When your child drops a four-letter word in your presence, try not to yell. Your child will definitely figure out that the word he used was a powerful one. Instead, find out where he heard it and explain why we don't use those words—especially in public.

Today, kids still learn taboo words on the school bus, but also on the Internet and TV, in music and magazines. They, too, have an incomplete grasp of the words—and lack the same understanding of the implications of using them. Ten-year-olds have asked me, "Ms. Levkoff, what's a dildo?" and "What's sixty-nine?"

When I coax them to tell me where they might have heard these words, the response is usually television. Even network TV is chockfull of sexual innuendoes and scenarios. It ain't just cable anymore! The dramas are steamier, the comedies are raunchier, and there's a voyeuristic genre—reality television—that didn't even exist when we were kids. Even dolls are sexier today. (I'm talking to you, Bratz.)

Childhood is indeed different these days, and we have a new responsibility to talk to our kids about the things that we hear, read, or see coming at them from all directions.

These at-home lessons should begin with their own bodies. My parents were diligent in discussing puberty with me, but I am not sure that I learned what the clitoris was (let alone that I had one) until I was eighteen and already having sex. And masturbation? Yeah, right. I thought that was something only boys did. (It was only recently that I finally understood what Cyndi Lauper's "She Bop" was all about.)

Whenever I have had the opportunity to work with kids, I make sure to teach a comprehensive unit on anatomy. Aside from loving the kids' responses—usually "Gross," "Do we have to?" and "Ugh"—I want this generation of boys and girls to have knowledge that most of us never had: a basic, matter-of-fact understanding of the penis and the vulva. Before you know it, the "ughs" have turned into "oohs."

One time I was explaining erections to a class: "It's very common and normal. Sometimes the penis feels hard and looks like it's standing up." As soon as I was finished, a little boy shot out of his seat. "Oh my God, is that what I get every morning? Wow! I'm not broken!" The rest of the boys added their own chorus of excitement and relief.

How invigorating and empowering plain and pure knowledge can be! We don't give children the credit they deserve. They are capable of learning and using this type of information as a foundation for building self-esteem, a positive body image, and a healthy sexual outlook and future. This ongoing education has to occur at home, in school, and, yes, on the school bus (as long as it is checked for accuracy).

I had my first run-in with sex education in the fifth grade. Permission letters were sent home a week prior to our one hour of sex ed.

Dear Parent,

Next week, your child will be participating in a lesson about puberty. He/She will be watching a video entitled _____ [the title depended upon your gender]. Please sign the permission slip at the bottom of the page and give to your child.

Sincerely,

Principal/Administrator

My mother signed the letter and I carried it to school like the rest of my mortified classmates. On the dreaded day, our gymnasium was split into two smaller rooms by an electric wall. The boys went to one side, the girls to another. I couldn't tell you what the boys were watching, but we learned about sanitary napkins. Yes, sanitary napkins! Our video, which I vaguely recall had something to do with a girl writing in her diary, showed us what happened to our ovaries with some simplistic animation. We were not excited. In fact, when the hour was over, the girls were pale-faced at the thought of a future of bulky Kotex and a wardrobe consisting of nothing but black pants.

The boys never learned about periods; we never learned about wet dreams. I believe some of the boys in our class didn't figure it all out until high school. The secrecy behind male and female development bred fear and mistrust of the opposite sex. Boys thought that periods were dirty, and we were horrified at the thought of seeing an erection.

Naturally, considering our ignorance, we were in for a rude awakening. I had my first experience with an erection when I was in the seventh grade. It belonged to a boy in my chorus class we'll call Max. One day, while we were standing in a circle at the front of the classroom (we were practicing in our respective vocal groups), it happened. Max developed an erection so powerful that to this day I can still visualize it. In the middle of "The Greatest Love of All," the giggling started and quickly swelled to a wave of hysteria. And then, the finger-pointing. "Look at Max—Max's got a boner! Max's got a boner!" the kids roared while our uptight chorus teacher looked on in horror. Max looked down at his sweatpants and saw what was protruding from them. Within seconds, his eyes welled up with tears. I was too embarrassed to look at Max, whose erection was pointing in my direction (seeing as though we were across from one another). Poor Max couldn't sit down; he couldn't leave for fear of running into someone in the hallway. He just stood there—feeling the greatest embarrassment of all time. If we didn't know what an erection was before that class, we sure did now.

Fifteen years later, our schoolmates still refer to Max as "the boy with the boner." As the mother of a boy, I am embarrassed by my class's reaction and for making Max feel so bad. Because at the end of the day, it could have happened to any of the boys. That's exactly what I told a class of ten-year-olds when they started chanting, "Brian has a boner, Brian has a boner," about a boy sitting in the front row. In fact, I doubt that Brian had an erection; they were just teasing him. But he was so embarrassed he asked if he could go to the bathroom. During those five minutes, I quietly chastised the boys for using "boners" to humiliate someone. As I explained, "Having an erection at an inconvenient time will happen to every single one of you at some point—it's only natural."

For these and many other reasons, I am dedicated to creating

Just for laughs, let me share my favorite question about menstruation. Upon hearing from an experienced classmate that a woman "bleeds" every month, one boy was curious about where all that blood goes. He looked around the room, deadpan, and asked, "What do you do? Stick a spoon under her tushy?" I will admit it was hard not to laugh, but I quickly set him straight—the spoon goes under the vaginal opening (I'm kidding).

Let's do what our gym teachers never did for us. Let's be straightforward with our kids. When boys get a chance to learn about women, we will be less scary to them later on in life. And perhaps these boys will grow up and feel comfortable running to the pharmacy to buy us tampons when we run out. But I won't hold my breath.

learning environments that are more comfortable than the ones I had as a child. Whether a sexuality class is coeducational—and I recommend that they are—there is no reason why boys should not know how the uterus sheds each month. As for girls, there are lots of things about the penis that we should know as well.

THE PROBLEM WITH "PRIVATE"

Most of us have been taught to label our genitals our "private parts," especially when we are in public. Though it is a widely used phrase, I question the rationale behind applying the term "private" to places we need to talk about. On a serious note, if a person were to touch us or our child inappropriately, we need the facts. If we continue to call these parts private, we might never learn about what goes on "down there." On a lighter note, how silly would our children sound if they grew up only calling their genitalia "my wiener," "my hoo-ha," or any other goofy word that we teach them because we are afraid of saying "penis" and "vulva." Now, this isn't easy—when you're used to slang your whole life, trying out "scientifically acceptable" terms may be a little embarrassing. But it's far less embarrassing than having a daughter who runs around talking about her "pootie tang."

I suggest forgoing the term "private" when explaining these parts to your children. You can acknowledge that they are "personal," but instead of conveying secrecy, which winds up suggesting that there is something wrong with speaking about them, try using adjectives like "special," "important," "great," even "unique." For example, "While all boys have penises, no two look exactly alike—yours is unique." Since most children, especially girls, grow up thinking that their parts are dirty or bad, changing this trend just might change the attitudes of a new generation of children.

THE DIFFERENCE BETWEEN THE BOYS AND THE GIRLS

Parenting, as you well know, isn't easy. So I often wonder why people aren't required to take a sex-ed class *before* becoming parents. Most of us haven't had a health class in more than twenty years, if that, and do you really remember what your middle-school gym teacher taught you? In an effort to bridge this sex-ed gap, I've created my own parental curriculum. Let's review.

GENITAL GLOSSARY

The Girls

Vulva: The vulva is the "official" name for the female genitals. It consists of the labia, the clitoris, the vaginal opening, the urethral opening, and the mons pubis (the fatty pad of skin that protects the pubic bone and genitals).

Clitoris: The clitoris is a small but powerful area of concentrated nerve endings at the top of the vulva where the labia meet. It is made from erectile tissue, similar to the penis. The clitoris is protected by a fold of skin called the clitoral hood. If stimulated, the clitoris is an area of great pleasure. (In fact, it is the only part of the body whose sole purpose is to provide pleasure.) Most women experience orgasms from the clitoris, not the vagina.

Labia: The labia are folds of skin that outline the sides of the vulva. There are two sets of them, called "minora" and "majora" (small and large, respectively). The labia serve to protect the vaginal opening. The labia majora is also where pubic hair grows during puberty.

Bartholin's glands: These are two small glands located on the labia minora that secrete fluid during sexual arousal.

Urethral opening: This is the opening of the urethra, the tube by which urine leaves a girl's body. At the other end it is connected to the bladder. (Make no mistake: girls urinate out of their urethra, not their vagina.) There are some women who can ejaculate; this fluid comes out of the urethra as well. While it exits the urethra, however, it is not urine.

Vaginal opening: The opening is the entranceway into the vagina, making it the only part of the vagina that can be seen from the outside. Menstrual blood, discharge (whitish fluid that the vagina produces to clean itself out), and a baby (if delivering vaginally) can come out of the vaginal opening.

The Boys

Penis: Do I really need to tell you what this is? Just in case you need a refresher, the penis is responsible for sending sperm into parts unknown. It is made from erectile tissue that will engorge when filled with blood.

Urethra: The tube inside of the penis that carries both semen and urine (though not at the same time). The urethra is connected to the bladder and crosses through the prostate gland to the opening at the head of the penis.

Scrotum: The scrotum is a sac of skin that protects the testes (testicles).

Foreskin: All boys are born with a foreskin, a piece of skin at the head of the penis. Some families choose to circumcise their male infants, which is the removal of foreskin. There is some evidence that circumcision offers protection against certain diseases, but for most families it is a religious or cultural rite of passage. Although they look different, circumcised and uncircumcised penises operate the same way and one is not better than the other.

THE REPRODUCTIVE SYSTEM

The Girls

Vagina: The vagina is the stretchy, muscular passageway inside of a woman's body. About a third of the way up the vagina there is a spongy area called the G-spot, which, if stimulated, can produce orgasms. (Not every woman can access this.)

Cervix: The cervix is the "neck" of the uterus, the lower portion that separates the uterus from the vagina. The opening of the cervix is called the *os.*

Uterus: The uterus is a pear-shaped stretchy muscle that plays a major role in female sexual development. Starting around puberty, the inner lining of the uterus, called the endometrium, thickens each month in order to provide a "cushion" for a fertilized egg. If there is no fertilized egg, the lining sheds and comes out of the cervix and the vaginal opening. This is called *menstruation* ("a period"). Though the uterus is commonly called "the womb," it should be noted that not every woman becomes pregnant and "uses" her uterus in this way.

Fallopian tubes: The fallopian tubes are responsible for carrying an egg to the uterus every month. If the fallopian tubes are damaged—by an untreated or progressive infection or disease—it can result in infertility or ectopic pregnancy (a pregnancy that develops outside of the uterus).

Ovary: The two ovaries (one on each side of the uterus) are responsible for estrogen production (the female sex hormone) and egg development. Each month, starting in puberty, one egg leaves one ovary and begins its travels through the reproductive system. If the egg isn't fertilized by sperm, it comes out of the vagina with the lining of the uterus, during menstruation.

The Boys

Testes: Testes (also called the testicles) are two oval organs that, beginning in puberty, produce testosterone (the male sex hormone) and sperm. The testes hang below the penis.

Epididymis: The coiled tube at the top of each testicle where sperm develop and mature.

Vas deferens: Two long tubes responsible for carrying sperm from each epididymis into the urethra. Sperm may also be stored in the vas deferens prior to ejaculation. (During a *vasectomy*, the vas deferens is cut and tied so that there is no sperm in semen, making a man unable to impregnate a woman.)

Seminal vesicles: Two pouches that supply energizing fluid (including the sugar fructose) to semen to aid sperm motility (ability to travel).

Prostate gland: The prostate secretes a milky white fluid that is an ingredient of semen. During puberty it grows to about the size of a walnut, but it may get bigger as a man reaches middle age. An enlarged prostate may require medical attention in adulthood.

Cowper's glands: Also called bulbourethral glands, these are two small glands that, during arousal, secrete a thick, clear fluid commonly called "precum" or preejaculatory fluid, which lubricates the urethra prior to ejaculation. (This fluid may contain sperm as well as transmit sexually transmitted diseases.)

> **D**id you know the penis and the clitoris come from the same embryologic tissue? Did you know the ovaries and testes start off the same too?

GROWING UP, OUT, AND MOODY

Puberty is the time when our child bodies develop and mature into our adult bodies. What complicates this time is that there are no rules. While everyone goes through the same types of emotional and physical changes, puberty is not a race and there is no clock. Everyone develops at their own pace—some earlier, some later. It is a process that takes years. A child does not wake up one day with an entirely new body and frame of reference.

The following table describes the changes that boys and girls experience as they go through puberty.

GIRLS	BOYS
Breast development	Erections become more common
Pubic hair	Pubic hair
Underarm hair	Underarm hair
Production of sex hormones	Production of sex hormones
Sexual feelings are more frequent	Sexual feelings are more frequent
Uterus and vagina grow larger	Penis and testicles grow larger
Eggs mature in the ovaries	Sperm is produced in the testicles
Menstruation begins	Wet dreams ("nocturnal emissions") begin
Body sweats more	Body sweats more
Nipples darken in color	Nipples darken in color
Skin and hair become oilier	Skin and hair become oilier
Growth spurt	Growth spurt
Hips widen	Chest and shoulders broaden
Voice changes	Voice "cracks" and begins to deepen
Weight gain	Weight gain
You may get pimples	You may get pimples
Breast muscles may ache	Breast muscles may ache
Grow nearly to full height	Chest and facial hair develop
Mood swings	Mood swings
Masturbation is common	Masturbation is common

Puberty can be equally traumatic for parent and child. Most children are desperate to "avoid" puberty—its name alone is strange and scary. Most parents are looking to wake up after it's over. I mean, who wants a moody preadolescent moping around? We often forget how tumultuous the emotional roller coaster can be. The physical turmoil during puberty is enough to drive someone mad. But instead, we are dealt a double whammy—the complications of emotional outbursts, identity confusion, and the complexities of your first crush. The drama of my own blossoming femininity is still vivid. I agonized over every crush and played cheesy ballads on my boom box until there were no more tears left to cry. Though my body may have become womanly, my head was too confused to make any adult decisions.

Physical changes during puberty are a given (no escaping from those), but there is no script for how to tackle the multitude of feelings that your child may have. He may go from happy to bitter to depressed all in a day, but it will get better. And though it may seem like you have a hormonal monster at home, after some time he will turn into your more mature and confident teen. It's hard to prepare for what your child may experience emotionally, but if we try to remember what it was like for us, we may be better able to sympathize with our kids.

Adolescence and puberty are not the same. Puberty refers to the process where a child's body becomes sexually mature and capable of reproduction. Adolescence refers to the transition, both emotional and physical, between childhood and adulthood. It is a state that has no definitive beginning or end.

FLASHBACK: WHAT DO YOU RECALL?

For most of us, puberty happened so long ago that we can barely remember it, and what we do remember isn't the physical changes—when we got our first pubic hair or whether or not our muscles ached—but the emotions, the angst, the hormones, and the endless crushes. And for your child, puberty is similarly his or her own private torture—especially without accurate information. But even though an overview of pubic hair, periods, and ejaculation is crucial, facts are not enough. Kids have a myriad of concerns about their bodies, their feelings, and their need to fit in. As parents, we need to do more than just provide the facts. We need to share our own experiences so that our kids can get some perspective and perhaps feel better about their own lives. They want to know all about your first crush, how you felt in those horrifying moments when you first realized you needed a bra, what you were thinking when you had your first wet dream and woke up with sticky sheets. Now is the time to revisit your past, because your future and your children's depend on it.

Kids learn how to cope from hearing how you faced and overcame the challenges of puberty. They begin to understand that they are not alone. You can share your stories with them in increments. If your child is starting to notice (and struggle with) slight breast

Kids have many anxieties about the way they look as they develop. Show your kids pictures of you during puberty. Let them see that puberty can be an awkward time for everyone—but they will get through it.

development, share with her how you or your friends handled this change. Take your time. You don't have to run right from breast development into what happens if you get your period in school, as this may make her more anxious. You are going to want to talk to her about all of those things, but follow her lead. And don't forget to talk to your children about the ages when you went through puberty, as some of them may experience some of the big changes at the same age you did.

Along these same lines, we should be talking about puberty to our children who aren't the same gender as us. While you might not know firsthand about menstruation or nocturnal emissions, your input is important. By ignoring the development of your "other gender" child, you implicitly put up a wall that says, "You are different from me. We can no longer touch, share, or bond as we once did." How silly does this sound? But it is our reaction to our children's development that shapes their sense of self.

Okay, this pseudo-lecture is mostly directed at fathers. Mothers are more likely to talk about puberty with their sons without completely falling apart. But fathers have an uncanny way of removing themselves, emotionally and physically, from their daughters as soon as breasts appear. Unfortunately, if you aren't offering her love or information, she will seek it from someone else. And you know that you want to be the one who provides your daughters with a healthy, loving male perspective. Her model for a loving interaction with the opposite sex is with her daddy. Fathers should make a concerted effort to be affectionate with their daughters during as well as after puberty. Your girls want to feel loved by you and won't necessarily understand why you are pulling away.

> **D**ads: Date your daughters! Do something special with them to let them know that you will always be in their lives. Spend a day for just the two of you. Go out to lunch, a museum, a game, or do something else that they love. Let them know that despite the physical changes taking place, your bond will only become stronger.

Though I, like many girls, didn't want the news of my first period traveling to my father, I am sure that within five seconds of my telling my mom about my newly found womanhood, she called him. When I came home from school the next day, there was a small box waiting on my bed. Inside was a ring and a card that read, "Even though you are now a woman, you'll always be my little girl. Love, Dad." To this day, it is perhaps the most vivid image I have of my experience with puberty. By acknowledging my first period, my father showed me that though I had changed, our relationship would not. Think about it. When you have an infant at home, both parents are involved in its daily care—even the one whose genitals differ from the baby's. Being a good parent doesn't end when the hormones kick in.

THE TRIALS OF EARLY DEVELOPMENT

For me and many others, being a girl was something we had to learn to love. While I relished the idea of being able to "do it all," a mantra perpetuated by my parents, there was something I couldn't do—control my body. That, I learned, nature was in charge of, and nature was calling (as it seemed to me, very early).

It happened the day before sixth grade began. I went to the bathroom, saw the surprise in my underwear, and promptly panicked. I knew what it was. I had read *Are You There God? It's Me, Margaret* and had the special "Mother-Daughter" lunch of tuna melts and French fries, and the obligatory dialogue about becoming "a woman." Even though I knew the benefits of womanhood—wearing eyeliner and lip gloss—I was still horrified. The walk from the bathroom to the kitchen on that Labor Day of 1987 was dreadful. "Um, Mom, I got my period." And then, she slapped me (in the customary Jewish congratulatory sort of way). I started to cry. Not because of the slap but because under no circumstance did I want this supposed gift that had been given to me.

Puberty shouldn't be a secret. Explain to all of your children what is going on. If your youngest child is curious about his or her siblings, explain it in simple terms: "Your sister/brother is going through puberty. They are becoming teenagers and are growing in new ways." And don't forget to tell your sons and daughters about the changes that their other-gender peers or siblings are experiencing!

Perhaps I should explain why I was so distraught about getting my period. I was—without a doubt—the first in my grade. My transition to womanhood had begun long before. Sometime in the fall of fifth grade my breasts appeared. There I was, this somewhat buxom five-feet-three-inch fifth-grader who had no idea what was going on with her body. I had a mouth full of braces, this horrendously ugly haircut, and breasts. While I was confused, everyone else was hysterical. The boys laughed, the girls laughed, and I am sure the teachers secretly pitied my early development. All of a sudden I felt guilty about being a woman.

> It's okay to be honest with your daughters about the pros and cons of periods. While there are lots of wonderful outcomes of getting older, including greater maturity and responsibility, menstruation is complicated. You can talk to children about the downsides, too, but just make sure that you balance out any negative information with the positives. We don't want them dreading or fearing this time in their lives.

When I was a girl, I was painfully aware that being a burgeoning woman meant being ostracized by your friends. As I developed, chants of "flirt," which at the time was synonymous with "slut," were all too common—even from my own circle of friends. As I attempted to understand my own body, my peers were making sure that I hated it as well. Call it envy, fear, or confusion, one thing is certain: Sometimes our friends can make going through puberty even more difficult.

THE RED SHIRT CLUB

When I was called in recently to speak at a particularly beautiful private school in a New York suburb, I encountered a phenomenon 180 degrees from my own experiences. In a world where overinvolved parents are de rigueur, the parents at this particular school were on a mission to protect their children from the teasing that they may have encountered during their own childhoods.

As the girls in one clique started menstruating, their mothers gave them bright red shirts (I assume to symbolize blood). The girls wore their red shirts with pride, proclaiming their womanhood on their chests. While these girls were shielding themselves from potential teasing, they wound up creating a new group of outcasts. The girls without breasts, underarm hair, or their periods felt left out and envious. The Red Shirts made peers feel unworthy, as if saying, "Ha! You aren't a woman yet. You are still a child."

Though I have worked with teens for some time, I was surprised by the role reversal and, for that matter, menstrual pride. Granted, having to wear red shirts is more a sign of immaturity than womanhood. The unsophisticated banner of menstruation is not womanlike at all. It is easy to don a cotton T-shirt. It is far more difficult to ponder the complexities of adulthood—the sexual feelings, desires, and range of emotions caused by raging hormones. But the lesson for us is very clear. Puberty takes time and individuals develop at their own pace. One is neither better nor worse than the other. Wherever a person falls along the girl–woman or boy–man spectrum is what is best for that individual. It is impossible, and unwise, to rush it.

S how your kids (boys too) what sanitary napkins and tampons look like and feel like. Let them stick them under water to see how they work. Verbal descriptions are just not sufficient for them to understand.

THE RISE OF BABY SUPERMODELS

I received an e-mail from a concerned parent that some of her daughter's fourth-grade friends were talking about "being fat." She had watched in horror as sixty-pound little girls tugged at their stomachs and said, "Why can't I get rid of this? I'm so fat." During our next class, when it was time to talk about puberty, I saw what she meant.

"Weight gain is a healthy and natural part of puberty," I explained. "As we become taller and as we begin to menstruate, our bodies need more weight to keep us healthy and strong." I watched a beanpole of a girl's mouth drop in shock. "I am not gaining weight. I want to be a supermodel," she announced to the class. With this, two other students began to describe the girl's diet of celery and carrots.

This is the direct result of years of watching parents and celebrities whittle themselves away for the sake of glamour and the ever-changing ideals of beauty. I explained that pubescent weight gain does not equal obesity, but it was as if I was talking to a brick wall. I was thrown by the girls' insistence that weight gain was not an option for them.

Fat, even a few well-needed pounds, was an evil thing that they believed would turn them into everything they fear. What they are learning about society's irrational standards of beauty will inevitably drain these girls of self-esteem, and in turn will drain them of what it means to be inherently, and beautifully, female— hips and all.

We can't control the overwhelmingly negative messages about

L et your children see how "beauty" has changed over the years. Show
them pictures of the *Venus de Milo*, Marilyn Monroe, and other men
and women in pop culture and history. Explain to your children that beauty
comes in many shapes and sizes and will continue to change and evolve
as they get older.

body images in our society, which is why it's so important for us to
combat them at home. We want to raise a new generation of healthy
and confident women who recognize that most people are not supposed to be a size zero. Our supermodels fluctuate from curvaceous
to emaciated. Our celebrities follow the same dieting techniques.
Television shows highlight the training regimens and eating habits
of the thinnest superstars. If we think that little girls and boys don't
watch these programs, we're wrong.

Boys are not immune to the body-image wars. I gave the same
information about weight gain during puberty to a class of sixth-
graders. A young boy, who was by no means fat but was perhaps a
few pounds heavier than his peers, responded with: "But you get
thinner, too. My mom said that I am going to get taller and lose
my fat." Now, I understand what she was trying to say, but talk
about giving your child a complex! Instead of supporting his current stature, she indirectly told him that he wasn't good enough
now, but would be someday. Both boys and girls need more than
we offer them. And is it a surprise? All of us have asked our partners, "Do I look fat?", ordered salads with dressing on the side,
and complained about our waistlines, whether they are actually

growing or not. Children see all; they hear all. Childhood obesity aside, all of us can do a better job supporting our children's physical selves.

COMPLICATED FEELINGS AND COMPLICATED RELATIONSHIPS

I thought that I matured early. But according to today's research, girls are developing as young as age seven or eight. In a 1999 study, it was not considered "abnormal" for girls to have pubic hair and breast development by the age of nine. I have seen it firsthand. Picture a class of boys and girls in the fourth grade. They are giggling during a discussion about wet dreams and ejaculations. There, sitting quietly and calmly, is a woman—at least in body. She is five feet two inches tall and has at least a C cup. If you saw her on the street you might think she was fifteen. She is respectful of her elders and her peers but never smiles when we begin to talk about menstruation. It is just too close to home, for this nine-year-old.

She is far more comfortable in her own skin than I ever was at that age. She walks with her head held high, even though she towers over all her classmates. I am proud to know her. Yet I worry about how others see her. You can tell, even during class, how the boys watch her. It wouldn't surprise me if adult men approached her regularly.

How can we teach people to understand that a mature body does not mean a mature understanding of sexuality? The struggle between mind and body is so difficult during puberty—at nine as well as sixteen. People make assumptions about sexual readiness when one's body appears to be in its sexual prime. People make assumptions simply by looking at the body of a young woman, no matter how old she is.

Yes, growing up is complicated by the presence of older suitors, especially when they offer a girl her first taste of sexual attention. When a young girl experiences new sexual feelings, they can be so overwhelming that it is easy to fall for an older person who shows her the slightest bit of interest. When your peers aren't appealing, seeing as they are still exploring other things, like snapping bras and shouting "Girls have cooties," an older person may seem like an appropriate partner.

I hadn't given much thought to this until I worked with a group of fifteen-year-old girls in Manhattan. At the end of our workshop, I asked them to write down any additional questions they had on an index card. Many of their questions were about statutory rape—what constituted it and what the age of consent was. I don't remember this ever being an issue when I was growing up. I couldn't tell you if I ever heard the term during my adolescence. But these girls were consumed with it. There were numerous questions: "How can it be rape if you love someone?" "What is statutory rape and are people really prosecuted for it?" "But what if I love him? Doesn't that matter? I wouldn't press charges." Of course, the decision to press charges or not lies with parents. It is our responsibility to act on these unequal relationships. And sometimes love has nothing to do with it. If parents feel like their children are being taken advantage of, they have the law on their side.

Teenage girls, in addition to being impressionable, are in the throes of puberty. Their bodies are still developing and their minds . . . well, we can all remember the emotional turmoil of our own youth. I was not even close to being sexually active at fifteen. In fact, it took a year for me to let a boyfriend touch my breasts over my shirt. If I had been having sex at that age, the emotional attachment would have been intense beyond my comprehension. I would have done anything for that person. And I am afraid that girls are doing just that. It is possible to have a wonderful and loving sexual relationship even at that younger age, but when two partners are not equal, how healthy can a relationship be? Can a teenage girl possibly have the strength to stand up to an adult partner? For sure, love is a complicated thing; it becomes more frightening when girls with womanly bodies become involved with men. (Dads, remember how I said that avoiding your daughters and their breasts has consequences? This is an unfortunate one. When you stop showing affection physically, girls sometimes seek it out from others.)

Just because more adult bodies have replaced childhood ones doesn't mean these children are adults. Explain to your children that they can still be kids even if they have facial hair or a period. Getting involved, sexually and emotionally, with someone who is older (and in many cases more "powerful") puts a teen in a difficult position if there's a need to negotiate. And by older, I don't mean a year older—I mean someone who is in a different stage of life or has different responsibilities and consequences for their actions. While the attention of someone older is appealing, an older person is not always the best partner for an impressionable teen.

AND IF YOU WERE WONDERING
ABOUT THE BOYS . . .

If you think that up to now this information has been girl-heavy, you are correct. The reason is that in all of my experiences, boys are far more comfortable talking about their bodies. But that doesn't mean that boys don't have insecurities about growing up. They do, though they are more likely to talk about them openly.

Boys are just younger men, so it shouldn't be a surprise that the most obvious puberty-related question from boys is about penis size. "How big are penises *supposed* to be?" We need to tell boys (and men) that there is no such thing as being the right size, nor is there any guarantee of how big their penises are going to become. Keep in mind that their exposure to media heightens the anxiety about penis size. Little boys are just as likely as you are to run across penis enlargement ads at the back of your favorite magazines. If that weren't enough, they are afraid that someone is going to make fun of them in the locker room when they are getting undressed. This anxiety may be due to size or whether or not your child is circumcised and "looks" like his peers. But circumcision is a choice and not a developmental issue, which you can explain to your son. For your son's other concern, there is no cut-and-dried answer (pardon the pun). We need to tell our children that puberty is a lengthy process. Some boys will develop early, some will develop later, but it is only a matter of time before everyone catches up. If your reassurance isn't enough, there may be a way for a boy who is really consumed by fear to get dressed in the bathroom stalls instead of at the lockers.

As for erections, I told you the story of Max, and you probably have your own similar story from childhood. Don't just tell your son that erections are normal; help him preempt the tricky situation of getting an erection in school, which will probably happen at some point, by giving him tips on how to avoid embarrassment. In my classes, I have told my students that if they get an erection in a group setting like the school hallway, they can hold a notebook in front of their pants until it goes away or (my students' favorite suggestion) they can run into the bathroom. Explain that an erection will go away in a few minutes if your son doesn't touch it. Suggestions like this will lessen the anxiety—even if boys never have to use them.

But there are some pubescent changes that a boy cannot control, like having a wet dream (or the scarier-sounding "nocturnal emission"). And while you might think that the fear is simply of having one, many boys have asked me, "Will I get into trouble for having a wet dream?" Of course not, right? I assure the boys that when parents have a son, there are some milestones that they are prepared to tackle, the first wet dream being one of them. But hopefully by now you have already spoken to him about these types of experiences so he won't be concerned with the possibility of getting grounded.

Last, physical development isn't just about the genitals. Growing up is also about our height, and needless to say, there are plenty of smaller boys who are eagerly anticipating their personal growth spurt. Reassuring them through this "waiting period," especially if they haven't grown yet, or don't grow to be that tall, can make the difference between self-confidence and complete insecurity. If you find yourself with a son who is upset by his height, talk to him about the many successful figures in our culture (music, film, television, and politics) who are not very tall—though you might want to leave out Napoleon because of that whole complex thing. These examples will show him that a person's worth isn't measured by his height, but by his character.

Boys get their own dose of sexual and body-related insecurities. They are told to be strong, muscular, and athletic at all costs. Professional athletes have admitted to steroid use, and some of this experimentation in the hopes of becoming "big" has trickled down to our own teenagers. On the sexual side, consider the Viagra and Levitra ads that plaster our billboards and air during every major sporting event. A class of seventeen-year-old boys worked with me recently in the hopes of understanding their own sexuality and that of women. One of the young men—at seventeen they are no longer boys—asked, "Are there any ways for us to have bigger and longer erections?" This was such a sad question from a male who was about to reach his sexual prime. We bombard them with messages of inadequacy. "Use supplements. Stay hard. Be a man. That's what she wants." They don't stand a chance with this type of messaging. And it's not as if little boys aren't receiving these insidious messages, too. More than a few ten- to twelve-year-old boys have asked me when they are "supposed" to start using Viagra—as if they will never be good or hard enough on their own. Let me make this clear: Boys aren't exempt from body-image anxiety. They just put up a tougher front.

IN THE END

If you set forth your values and speak early and frequently, you should breeze right through puberty. Just kidding. Puberty is never

> I was teaching a fourth-grade class when a little girl asked shyly, "Will we be talking about periods?" There were two minutes left until the bell rang so this was a very inopportune time to provide important information. I responded, "Yes. We will be discussing what a period is during the next class. If you can hold your questions until then, that would be great!" Unfortunately, a boy looked up and yelled, "What's a period?" As I started to repeat, "Hold your quest—" it happened. Another girl called out, "It's when your privates bleed!" The boy squealed and grabbed his groin. And then the bell rang and there was no time left to explain.

a breeze, but for the parent who has the right ammunition, it isn't as bad as you think. And just to help you out, here are some of the questions, with answers, that your kids will probably ask at some point during their development.

10 Common Questions About Anatomy and Puberty Children and Teens Want Answers To

1. **WHAT ARE THE THREE HOLES OF THE VAGINA?**
   The vagina doesn't have three holes. The vulva has two "holes"—the urethra (where urine exits) and the vaginal opening (the entrance to the vagina). The third "hole" is the anus.

2. **WHAT IS THE DIFFERENCE BETWEEN THE VULVA AND THE VAGINA?**
   The female genitals (including the clitoris, the labia, the vaginal opening, and the urethra) are called the vulva. The vagina is the

passageway inside the female reproductive system. Menstrual blood, discharge, and a baby can come out of the vagina.

3. **SOMETIMES MY TESTICLES FEEL LIKE THEY ARE HANGING LOW . . . WHY?**

In order to produce sperm, the testicles need to be at a particular temperature. If you are sweaty and overheated, your testicles will hang lower to "cool off." If your body is too cold, you might find that your testicles hug closer to your body.

4. **AT WHAT AGE DO BOYS DEVELOP THEIR SPERM?**

Sperm production begins during puberty. And you never know exactly when it is going to begin. On average, boys start going through puberty around the age of eleven.

5. **WHAT IS THE HYMEN?**

The hymen is a thin tissue that partially blocks the opening of the vagina. Many children and teens ask about the hymen because it relates (in their minds) to virginity. Sadly, the old phrase "popping a cherry" still exists, and kids are confused about what that really means. Though a girl may tear her hymen during sexual intercourse, many girls tear their hymens long before that—and don't even notice it. The presence of a torn hymen is not a good indicator of a loss of virginity.

6. **WHERE IN THE WOMAN'S BODY DO ORGASMS COME FROM?**

Most of women's orgasms come from the clitoris, though some women experience vaginal orgasms.

7. **WHAT IS A PERIOD?**

The menstrual cycle controls our fertility. Once a month, an egg is released from one of the two ovaries. As the egg travels toward the uterus, the uterine lining develops a thick cushion in case a pregnancy occurs. If sperm doesn't fertilize this egg, however, the uterine lining sheds and the egg, the lining, and some blood come out of the vagina. This is called menstruation or a period.

8. WHEN DO GIRLS GENERALLY GET THEIR PERIODS?

Though there is no one age when a girl gets her first period, typically, a girl experiences underarm hair, some breast development, and discharge (white fluid that comes out of the vagina) before she menstruates.

9. WHAT IS THE CLITORIS?

The clitoris is a bundle of sensitive nerves at the top of the vulva where the labia meet. The clitoris is very similar to the penis in that it is made of erectile tissue and feels good when touched.

10. HOW MANY TIMES A DAY CAN BOYS HAVE ERECTIONS?

During puberty, a boy can have many erections a day. Sometimes erections happen when least expected. Though it can be embarrassing, it is very normal.

Chapter Four

MASTURBATION: WHY BOYS DO AND SOME GIRLS DON'T

"IS MASTURBATION SOMETHING THAT HURTS?"

When one of my nine-year-old students asked this question, I wasn't really surprised. When I was nine (pre–sex career), I wouldn't have known either. Growing up, I didn't really understand what masturbation meant. It was an odd word, spelled strangely, and rarely mentioned, if at all. My friends who had brothers were probably better versed in masturbation—if not in actually doing it, in understanding that it existed. A boy locking himself in his bathroom for an extra-long shower is commonplace in many families, but seeing as I didn't have a brother, I didn't really get it.

By the time I figured out what masturbation meant, I was pretty sure that it only had to do with boys. I had no reference and no idea that females could do it at all. I only learned different when I participated in a high school HIV prevention workshop that explained the safer sex benefits of mutual masturbation. I would like to say that times are different today and that we have learned that self-stimulation is a natural and gender-free behavior, but no such luck. There still appears to be a gender divide when it comes to masturbation.

A few years ago I was asked to speak to a senior leadership class at a suburban high school. The students were a few months away from going to college and, as it turns out, desperate for information.

After a heated discussion about safer oral sex and other health-related items, a young man cautiously raised his hand. "I am not sure if I should ask this, but why don't women admit to masturbating?" The boys in the class started to cheer him on. In a split second he went from hesitant to confident. Responding to the cheers, he added, "I mean, c'mon, we know they all do it." Immediately, the girls became incredibly uncomfortable, flustered, and indignant.

Though I hoped that the girls would rise above their embarrassment to answer the boy's question, or even challenge it, the room remained silent and I was forced to jump in. My first priority (and in general, ours as parents) was to assure this young man that his question had value. "Even though the girls are quiet, that is a great question! Masturbation is one of those topics that none of us talk about as much as we should. But let's get one thing straight. Not every woman does it. Not every man does it either. It's interesting to explore why some people don't masturbate and why some who do aren't able to admit it." Perhaps part of this student's assumption about girls and masturbation stemmed from his personal experience with masturbation. It was such a frequent and natural activity for him—how could it not be for girls?

Teenage boys aren't the only curious ones. In the midst of a discussion on the subject, a ten-year-old boy raised his hand and asked, "What is it called if a girl masturbates?" When he learned that it was the same word, he continued. "Does *Playboy* help women to masturbate too?" He didn't have any doubt girls masturbated; he just wanted to know how they did it. (Let's be honest, don't grown men want to know the same thing?)

Girls rarely ask questions about male masturbation (except if the question is: "What's the point of giving a hand job if boys can do it [and frequently do] themselves?"). But boys of all ages do have questions. Many of my male students are interested in learning about female sexual response—probably more so than young women. Young boys are curious about what makes girls different from them, and older boys (and young men) are concerned with how women function because they want to become generous and competent partners and lovers (though the last label may be frightening to hear as a parent, it is not a bad characteristic for a man to have).

The concept of masturbation and orgasm is fascinating to all of us, at all ages. A ten-year-old boy once asked me, "What triggers orasm?" (Yes, orasm—he didn't know there was a g in the word.) The kids in the class didn't even know what that word meant. He told them, "When sperm comes out," to which the class responded in unison, "Ohhh. . . ." But I had to challenge them—that's not what an orgasm is, though you can already see the assumption developing that orgasms are male in nature.

Boys are definitely better schooled in all things masturbatory, and I have asked many girls why they, as a gender, aren't as well versed (so to speak) as boys. The most common answer seems to be purely anatomical. The fact that boys actually have to hold their penises when they urinate sets them up for a better understanding of their genitals. What boy doesn't know what (or where) his penis is?

"It's an outside-inside thing," said one fourteen-year-old girl. Really? Because I thought that the clitoris was on the outside of a woman's body—it isn't inside the vagina. For sure, there is a great deal of misunderstanding. A parent once asked me, "Do you think it's appropriate to suggest to girls that they use a mirror to look at their genitals?" Yes! It is a *great* idea. If we don't look at ourselves, we can go for years before we realize that our genitals are even attached to us at all. Have you seen yours recently? Sadly, I suggested this to a class of teenagers recently and they looked at me as if I had six heads, which is actually kind of heartbreaking.

Even though I pride myself on being tolerant of every person's sexual choices, frankly I am concerned for the girls who act out sexually but *don't* masturbate. They may be happy to give a hand job or blow job, but the idea of touching their own genitals is, according to one girl I spoke with, "nauseating." So the parts you were born with make you nauseated, but putting someone's penis in your mouth is cool? I mean, really, of all the things to make you gag, it would seem fairly obvious that oral sex could, quite literally, be one of them.

Consider another class of high school freshman girls. Some of them were sexually active—orally and vaginally—and deemed themselves well versed in sex. In a lesson on female sexual response, I asked them where the majority of women's sexual pleasure comes from. On cue, they responded, "The clitoris." But when I asked where it was, they couldn't tell me! So I decided to whip out some vulva diagrams and pass them around. The girls mouthed "gross" to each other as they took one and handed the stack to the student next to them. The last girl to get the handouts walked over to my desk to deposit the extras and dropped them facedown. Facedown! It was a clear example of how reluctant teenage girls are to look at their own bodies, even when they aren't afraid of using them.

Throughout history, masturbation—and sexual pleasure as a whole—has been condemned as a "forbidden" behavior. Children caught masturbating were sometimes forced to wear preventive devices that could double as tools of torture. The remnants of this antimasturbation movement are guilt, shame, and a resulting inability to admit that we take part in, and even enjoy, masturbating. What were you told growing up? Do you remember a time when you were "caught" or told not to masturbate because something terrible would happen to you? If your experience with masturbation (or learning about it) was negative, you may feel unable to tackle the subject with your own children. But there is nothing wrong with telling your children it is okay to do. Take a look at the old myths. Aren't you glad that we now know better and don't have to terrify our children with the thought of becoming a blind wolfman?

Hairy palms: How many people have you seen walking around town with furry palms? I am pretty sure that this old scare tactic doesn't work that well today.

Going blind: According to certain surveys, 62 percent of females and 92 percent of males masturbate (Kinsey, 1953/1998; Kinsey, 1948/1998). Even if only 50 percent of people masturbated regularly, you would expect to see a whole lot more visually impaired people in the population. This myth may have arisen because eyesight starts to change around puberty, which is also when masturbation becomes very frequent.

Using up your sperm: I would say that one of a boy's greatest concerns is whether his masturbatory habits will permanently damage his reproductive system, most specifically his ability to "make" a girl pregnant. Masturbation will not wreak havoc on your fertility. The testicles produce millions of sperm regularly, and will continue to do so ad infinitum.

Masturbation is only for the young: The idea that masturbation is only for the young does a disservice to all of us wherever we are in our lifespan. Masturbation is just as healthy during adulthood as it is in youth. The difference is that adult masturbation is commonly accompanied by more sophisticated sexual fantasies. It is important for children to know that there are ways of being sexual regardless of your age or whether you have a partner.

THE MISSING MESSAGE

We spend so much time getting our toddlers not to touch themselves in public that we often forget to give them the positive message, too. But masturbation is a large component of our sexual development. Even fetuses touch their genitals in utero, and male fetuses have erections in utero as well. Body-related curiosity is innate, and not something to be ashamed of. In the past, when I have told kids that masturbation is a behavior that both boys and girls participate in, for the most part they too are surprised. Even at the age of twelve, many kids think that masturbation is a male word and a strictly male activity.

As parents, we should be telling our children that it is completely normal to be curious about our bodies and to want to explore all of our parts. This lesson can begin when they are toddlers and are quite demonstrative about what they are doing beneath their diapers or when they are naked. This creates a positive attitude around masturbation (and their bodies in general) that they may better understand as they get older. If your children are older, you can tell them that as they go through puberty they will want to touch their genitals for many different reasons, including to see how their parts have developed and to experience pleasure. You should assure them that there is nothing wrong with doing so—whatever their motivation. There doesn't need to be a huge discussion and we don't need to show children "how to do it." But we should teach them about anatomy and allow them to figure it out for themselves.

It seems to me that masturbation is perhaps the safest sex we can have. (Because you know what? Abstinence isn't sex.) I am not alone in this belief. Many educators and parents believe the same thing. Alas, one of the most famous physicians-turned-sex-educators, Dr. Joycelyn Elders, had to resign from her post as Surgeon General because she said so. It is certain that the act of masturbation is often chastised because of its religious implications. You know, that whole "man should not spill his seed" thing and "no sex outside of marriage." But does masturbation truly count as sex? And what about women? Since women don't spill seed, I guess they must be free to do whatever they want! That reminds me of a question boys and girls often ask. Once they find out that the testicles are producing millions of sperm starting at puberty, they want to know if they are supposed to have millions of kids. Obviously the answer is no.

So the children bring up a good point . . . a controversial one, but a good one. If boys are not supposed to have millions of kids, what are they supposed to do with all that extra sperm?

Young children will ask you if everyone masturbates. Tell them the truth—some do, some don't—and you can even share with them the different religious and cultural values that surround masturbation. Sexuality is a sensitive subject for many groups. Though children may hear that masturbation is sinful, they must be taught that it is a completely safe behavior. Hopefully, this conversation can initiate a greater dialogue about diversity—though you should always emphasize the facts over the values. Masturbation is healthy for someone to engage in, no matter what we have heard or what some people believe.

WHAT'S A GIRL TO DO?

I am not suggesting that we all tell our daughters to go out and buy vibrators—though if you do, that's fine, too—but we need to start telling women that they are not built like men. They are entitled to receive sexual pleasure. Scratch that—it is *important* that women receive sexual pleasure, especially when it comes from their own hands. If a woman doesn't masturbate, what happens to her if she never receives pleasure with a partner? Or what if she does and becomes dependent upon someone else for pleasure? Moreover, women who don't masturbate may have unrealistic expectations of what sex is all about. Many women expect that sex, even sex for the first time, is going to produce mind-blowing orgasms. In addition to this being unlikely, it sets women up for disappointment.

When women don't receive pleasure from sex, we are quick to label it as "sexual dysfunction." The truth is, if we really understood how females experience pleasure—and from where on the body they get that pleasure—we might not have women experimenting with random herbs, supplements, and drugs in a quest for better orgasms. There are real dysfunctions out there, but we seem to be quick to medicalize female sexuality instead of actually talking about it.

We have made some headway in the discussion of sexuality and pleasure. Mass media—even our prime-time shows—are starting to refer to female masturbation and the tools women commonly use during it. *Everwood, Sex and the City,* and who knows how many reality shows have referenced vibrator use. So whether we choose to believe it or not, our kids know what vibrators are, and some of our teens own them. Though this may seem horrifying, there may be worse things for them to know about. The fact is women are built differently than men, and a lot of us, both men and women, seem to forget it and lead our own pleasureless lives. If adults can't remember, how can we possibly help our children when they are getting mixed messages from a multitude of sources?

Going by movies and television, you would think that every sexual encounter would lead to intense pleasure, but in reality the majority of women don't have orgasms from intercourse alone. Female genitals are complex and we don't talk about them very often. One out of every three e-mails I receive from women of all ages concerns their inability to have orgasms during sexual intercourse. (I know what you're thinking—what on earth does this have to do with my child, right now? I promise, there is a point here.) Boys are taught, implicitly and explicitly, that sex will end in orgasm for them. They will always have pleasure—simply because of how their genitals function. Girls are not so lucky. Because they aren't told anything different, they assume that they are supposed to feel something good during sex and are often disappointed, frustrated, or even shamed when they don't.

A girl who's disappointed may chalk it up to a partner who isn't that skilled in the romantic arts. Too many others blame themselves for not having the "right" response. Either way, more knowledge would alleviate the insecurities that girls may feel about their own bodies and their capacity to be sexually satisfied.

If a girl doesn't masturbate and receives pleasure for the first time at the hands of a partner, she may assume that this is the only way for her to have an orgasm, and seek out partners instead of using her innate power. And then there are other girls who seek out partners in the hopes of finding the magic one that will make her feel like one of those women in the movies—the ones who can experience orgasms. Truth be told, I would much rather these girls learn that they can do it on their own; they don't need someone else.

During an eleventh-grade health seminar, I asked my class of all girls if they were ever the recipients of oral sex. They said that typically they did not "receive," but if they did, it was rare that they got any pleasure from it. Why? Because according to this class, "girls take longer to be comfortable with their bodies." I believe that it is a girl's lack of personal knowledge about her own body (and its natural abilities and potential for pleasure) that send girls out into the world feeling ashamed, more likely to provide pleasure instead of receive, and inevitably feel unfulfilled.

If we are looking to empower both males and females it is our duty to explain that they need to be comfortable with their bodies as well as their minds. This is tricky, as we don't want our children to put all of their self-worth in the physical, but feeling good about their bodies is part of becoming healthy individuals. Without knowledge, this is virtually impossible.

THE BENEFITS OF SELF-LOVE

Yes, it turns out that masturbation is good for you. Can you believe it? And the benefits of masturbation are far greater than "It just feels good."

1. Masturbation is an effective way for anyone to understand their body and what feels good. This makes us less likely to rely on a partner to provide pleasure. It also allows us to effectively communicate with sexual partners because we know what makes us feel good.
2. Masturbation may be an effective way of staying abstinent. By masturbating, we rid ourselves of sexual tension and don't feel compelled to act out sexually through oral, anal, or vaginal intercourse. There is no risk of contracting a sexually transmitted disease or becoming pregnant through masturbation.
3. Masturbation is relaxing. It offers stress relief and muscle relaxation, and can be sleep-inducing.
4. Masturbation can reduce menstrual cramps. The muscle contractions that occur during orgasm can alleviate cramping and other discomfort.

5. Masturbation aids in the release of mood-elevating hormones. During orgasm, endorphins are released into the bloodstream and we become, for lack of a better word, happy.

6. Masturbation may reduce the risk of prostate cancer. Recent studies have found that males who ejaculated on a regular, frequent basis had lower rates of prostate cancer than those who didn't (Leitzmann, et al., 2004; Giles, et al., 2003).

AND IF YOU FIND YOUR CHILD MASTURBATING?

It's probably going to happen at some point. While it may seem like the worst thing in the entire world, you will survive. Whatever age your child is, try not to make a big deal out of it. The more attention you bring to the behavior, the more likely you are to send the message that this is an earth-shaking, and perhaps problematic, behavior. If your young child is touching himself you might want to encourage him to go to his room so that he can have privacy. ("Honey, why don't we find a private place for you to do this?") If he asks you, "Why does it have to be private?" let him know that masturbation should be a pleasurable activity done in a quiet, personal space, such as his room; it's like going to the bathroom—not everyone feels like watching. Masturbating in private respects other people's feelings.

The key to handling a child masturbating is to not panic. If we freak out, we do more damage than good. And if you walk in on your adolescent, simply say excuse me and leave. From then on it will remind you that you should knock before entering your teen's room.

**10 Common Questions About Masturbation
Children and Teens Want Answers To**

1. **IS IT OKAY IF I MASTURBATE MORE THAN ONCE A DAY?**

   People should do what makes them feel good and comfortable. Nothing bad will happen if a child is masturbating twice a day. If he or she is masturbating so much that it interferes with social life or school work, however, there is a problem that needs to be addressed. But health-wise, there is really no such thing as too much masturbation.

2. **WHAT DOES SEMEN LOOK LIKE?**

   Semen is a mixture of sperm, several different fluids, and proteins. It's milky white and sticky. If a man ejaculates more than one time a day, fewer sperm is present in each ejaculation, so his semen may seem more watery than before.

3. **WHEN A PERSON EJACULATES, HOW MUCH SPERM COMES OUT?**

   When a male ejaculates, about one to three teaspoons of semen come out.

4. **DOES EJACULATION HURT?**

   It does not hurt. The feelings you get when you ejaculate are very pleasurable.

5. **WHAT IS AN ORGASM?**

   Orgasms are intensely pleasurable feelings that come from muscle contractions in the genitals. Masturbation is one way that people can experience orgasms.

6. **IS IT TRUE THAT WOMEN START TO MASTURBATE AFTER HAVING SEX FOR THE FIRST TIME?**

When it comes to personal behaviors, no two people are alike. Some women may masturbate after becoming sexually active, some women may have masturbated since they were little girls, and some women don't masturbate at all.

7. **IS IT HEALTHY TO MASTURBATE? IF YOU DO IT TOO MUCH CAN YOU BECOME IMPOTENT LATER ON IN LIFE?**

It is completely natural and normal to masturbate. You cannot become impotent later in life because of how often you masturbated as a child.

8. **WHEN WILL I GET ERECTILE DYSFUNCTION?**

Though this appears unrelated to masturbation, boys may ask this because they realize that masturbation should produce (at least) an erection. Because there are so many advertisements for erectile dysfunction (ED) medications, some boys assume that ED will happen to them at some point in their lives, and needless to say, they are nervous. Erectile dysfunction refers to a condition that some men may develop as they get older. When a man has ED, he has difficulty getting and maintaining an erection. It is important to tell your children that ED refers to an adult condition and isn't something they need to worry about now. We don't want to mock their question, but it is better to focus on developmental changes they will *definitely* experience now.

9. **CAN YOU GET AN STD FROM MASTURBATION?**

Masturbation is considered a safe sexual activity. Of course, for general hygiene reasons, after masturbating (or touching someone else) children and teens should know that they should wash their hands.

10. WHAT IS THE AVERAGE TIME IT TAKES FOR A PERSON TO HAVE AN ORGASM?

That depends on the person. Some people may take a few minutes; others much longer. Many times this question is asked because teens are concerned with being "normal." It is important to explain to them that whatever is "normal" for them may not be the same for someone else—and that's okay. Every person is different. There are some people who can reach orgasm quickly, and others who take a while. But in many cases, the time it takes for people to have an orgasm is also affected by how well they know their body, too.

Chapter Five

SEXUAL ORIENTATION

I didn't know much about homosexuality as a child. I couldn't tell you what "gay" meant, but I did know it had a negative connotation and it was something no one talked about in public. Our culture was consumed with antigay sentiment (just think of the Reagan administration and its self-imposed gag order on the word "AIDS"). Right before my eleventh birthday, I had my first run-in with the subject of sexual orientation. We were driving to Vermont to visit my dad's family. My father said, "We need to talk to you about something."

"Am I in trouble?"

"No, sweetheart. We just need to talk to you," my mom reassured me.

Quickly, and without any additional emotion in his voice, my father said, "Your aunt is gay and lives with another woman. We thought that it was time that we told you." He looked at me and waited for my response.

"Well . . . I . . . can I catch it?" I asked, even though I really didn't understand what all the fuss was about.

"No, Logan, it's nothing you can catch."

"Okay," I replied. I really wasn't concerned that my aunt was gay. She didn't like boys. I got that. But I was worried about what my friends would say if they found out. We didn't talk about "gay" back then. Scratch that: We talked about gay men and AIDS, but that was about it. Lesbians were not part of a larger public dialogue, and I wasn't sure how my peers would react. Looking back, I'm disappointed to have reacted that way. But I was eleven and didn't know any better—and my reaction was (and still is) representative of how adolescents think.

> Ask your children to define what a "family" is. Explore the different types of families that exist (for example, single mother, stepparents, two moms, two dads, grandparents, a mom and a dad), and while you certainly should include gay families, you can also talk about how friends can be part of our families, too.

Kids are self-centered and care most about how something affects them. In addition, our immediate response to those who are different is often purely instinctual—it makes us uncomfortable, even when, as with others' sexual orientation, it has absolutely nothing to do with us. While urban environments may be somewhat tolerant of diversity, suburban schools are less forgiving. At least, that has been my experience, both personally and professionally. As a junior in high school, I attended a pro-choice rally during a college tour. The organizers of the event gave away stickers emblazoned with "Support Vaginal Pride" in giant purple and white letters. I thought nothing of putting this sticker on the front of my loose-leaf binder.

Seemingly within moments, the rumors began. "Did you hear that Logan is a lesbian?" Stories swirled through the hallways about my supposed affair with a friend. Three years later, my closest friend at college, who as it happened attended a neighboring high school, revealed that she too had heard the rumor—and initially had been afraid to meet me.

Being gay today, especially as a teenager, can still be devastatingly difficult. Some of the most wrenching conversations I have had have been with teens who are starting to identify as gay, lesbian, or bisexual. Perhaps the most poignant of these dialogues happened when I was asked to speak to the senior health classes back at my old high school. I was hoping that the social climate had changed since I was there.

When I went back to high school, so to speak, I learned how tough it still is to be an outsider—especially a gay outsider. During one of my lectures, I watched a young man in the corner of the room. Every time he spoke, someone snickered. Finally, he fell silent—even though I'd sent some of his classmates out of the room. When class was over, he waited for me outside the door. "Ms. Levkoff, do you know what it's like to be the only gay kid in school? They torture me."

Of course I didn't know. But I could provide him with some

resources that would help him get by during this difficult time, including Web sites for teens needing extra guidance and support. I tried to tell him that things would get better—but I knew that until he got out of that small town, with that small-town mentality, life would not be easy.

Another teen I know, whom I'll call Jon, has regaled me with examples of homophobia at his school. While he himself is trying to be tolerant and open-minded, he's surrounded by the antigay sentiments of his peers. (There is an important distinction between gay men and women. In high school—as well as in our own media—lesbians are often considered "cool" and "sexy.") This "mob mentality," so indicative of peer pressure in high school, was something that he was hesitant to speak up against. He was afraid that his friends would ostracize him for challenging them.

But there had been a time when he was not so open-minded. For months he and I debated the issues of sexual orientation. He was convinced that gay men were an unacceptable part of society. Over and over, I explained the reasons sexual orientation was an important and innate part of one's life and that gay men were entitled to the same respect as heterosexual men. Try as I did, he wouldn't budge. He was as homophobic as one could be without acting out physically.

Three weeks after our last heated debate I heard from Jon via instant message. He wrote, "Logan, remember when you gave me all those reasons why gay people were okay and normal?" (Out of context, I must admit this sounds very strange).

Considering I had used my entire intellectual arsenal to debate him, I wrote back, "I told you a lot of things. Are you thinking of something in particular?" It turned out that he was asking me to give him *all* the reasons why we should accept gay men. Although I was somewhat overwhelmed by the task, I sensed that this was urgent. I asked him, "Can I make some notes for you tomorrow?"

Jon wrote back immediately, "No." His explanation made me simultaneously sad and proud. "We are talking about sexual orientation in health class tomorrow. Most of the people in my class are homophobic. I want to give your information to my teacher so that he can tell the class. I am not comfortable saying it myself." Talk about teen angst! Jon was nervous about being the isolated voice within his peer group, but wanted his class to get the information— even if he couldn't provide it himself. His was only one voice, and an anonymous one at that. But if more teens are like that, there is hope for our future.

> If you hear your kids use the phrase "That's so gay," ask them to explain what they mean. Then suggest that they choose a new word, one that has nothing to do with a group of people, to express what they're trying to say!

THE SCHOOL TRIP

I have always tried to push the envelope in my unconditional support of tolerance and acceptance. But my finest hour, the best stunt I ever pulled, took place long before my career in sexuality began. It would have hardly been recognized if not for a phone call my mother received. The call was from my aunt. She was frantic. "Susan, are you and Steven getting divorced? Is there something you need to tell me?"

I can imagine the shock on my mother's face as my aunt continued. "Sue, there is a rumor that you and Steve are gay." What?

At the time, I was away on a Model Congress trip along with my fellow debaters. We would act as senators and representatives, writing, passing, vetoing, and arguing over bills. My bills were always the social advocacy kind—legalizing prostitution, promoting women's rights, and supporting gay marriage.

The third day of our trip, hundreds of students gathered to publicly defend their bills. The first bill on the docket was the bill to legalize gay marriage. (This was about a dozen years before it came up in the real world.) The college student running the forum asked for someone to speak in favor of the bill. No one raised a hand, except for me. I got out of my seat and walked to the center of the room. In front of my schoolmates and the entire Model Congress delegation from the East Coast, I had to make my case.

Legalizing gay marriage was more complicated than claiming that everyone was entitled to civil rights. I needed something better. I needed something bold. That's when it hit me. I stood up in front of the crowd of wide-eyed teenagers and said: "Perhaps we fear gay marriages because we don't know anyone who is the product of one. Let me be the first to tell you that my parents' marriage is one of convenience. Both my mom and dad are gay, and although they live together, they have long-term lovers outside of our home. I am proud of my parents and I have turned out just fine. If we legalize gay marriages, we give people like my parents an opportunity to celebrate their true loves."

I don't know where it came from, but it got a great reaction from the crowd. I strutted back to my seat, smiled at my schoolmates, who I assumed would understand the hoax, and watched as the bill passed with flying colors. I was a huge success!

Two days later, when our bus pulled into the high school parking lot, I barely gave any thought to my artificial "outing." I crawled into my parents' car and lay down on the backseat.

"Logan, do you need to tell us something? Did you tell anyone that your father and I were . . . gay?"

"Oops . . . I mean, who told you that?"

It seemed people in small towns gossip even when they are away from home. A boy in my school called his mother to tell her the news of my parents' homosexuality. Apparently, this started a telephone chain of grand proportions. And yes, eventually word got to my aunt. I told my parents of my performance and braced for their commentary.

"Logan, I think that was fantastic! Good for you," my father replied. "I am so proud of you. You know exactly what it takes to get your point across." My mother began to laugh in the front seat, and I went home feeling accomplished.

All my life, I have given a great deal of thought to what sexual orientation really means. My Model Congress speech was heartfelt, even if the specifics were fictional. But sexuality isn't so black and white. It isn't and never has been as simple as "gay or straight." We are fortunate to be complex creatures that can turn on to a variety of experiences and people. We are not limited; we can be liberated.

Adults have a hard time understanding this; kids do, too. Our sexual orientation doesn't miraculously reveal itself to us at a particular age. Sometimes we know when we are young; sometimes it takes years to figure out who we really are. And some kids experiment with the same sex when they are young while remaining heterosexual in their sexual orientation. It is innocent curiosity—nothing more.

Researchers have worked hard to determine where "gay" comes from—it may be neurological or genetic; it may even be part of hormonal development in utero. But if we don't know exactly "where," we know the answer to "when"—before birth. Homosexuality is not a choice. And the places and programs that claim to be able to "turn you straight" are, quite frankly, without a scientific leg to stand on.

When speaking to children I often compare it to one's first crush. How did you know that you liked someone? Did you wake up one morning and say, "Today I am going to like Adam, or Melissa?" Was it a conscious, thought-out decision? Or did you just know, deep down in the pit of your stomach, that you liked the object of your affection? We do not choose whom we are attracted to. We can choose whom to *sleep* with, but that isn't the same thing as romantic or even sexual attraction.

Come on, I hear you asking, if a man has sex with another man, doesn't that make him gay or at least bisexual? Technically, unless someone identifies himself as gay, it isn't our right to label him that way. Sexual orientation refers to who we are sexually attracted to. Though we can act out sexually with anyone, no one can tell us what we are feeling inside. This is probably the most complicated subject to explain to a child, but it is something that we should all keep in mind. And perhaps, if we were more tolerant of diversity and less caught up with labeling others, this really wouldn't be an issue.

There is no doubt that we live in a heterosexist world. We assume that everyone is straight, and that it is okay to make presumptions about other people and their sexual lifestyles. Thankfully, not everyone is straight and there is diversity wherever we look. (And by the way, though I use the term "straight," I question that too. What on earth is that supposed to mean?) While we may not understand or agree with an individual's sexual choices, we should be teaching our children about tolerance and respect. At the end of the day, does a person's sexual orientation affect us directly? The latest political action regarding gay marriage is one of those landmarks that will have an impact on the way we look at relationships in the future. Certain states' decisions to provide marriage— and not civil unions—to gay couples make a bold statement. Our world is changing.

I was asked by an astute nine-year-old, "If gay really means happy, why do people make fun of gay people?" Unfortunately, there is no good answer to that question. There has never been a reason to treat people with disrespect. Homophobia is as bad as any other type of hatred—including racism and religious persecution. People should be judged according to their character, not who they sleep with.

I'm particularly disturbed by how many people now use "gay" to mean "uncool" or "unacceptable," the way previous generations misused the words "spastic" or "retarded." Listen to a group of kids for ten minutes and inevitably someone will toss out the word "gay" as an insult—even when no one is referring to sexual orientation.

Ask your children how they would feel if their name became the "in" slang for something stupid or uncool. While using certain words doesn't automatically make them prejudiced, they do need to be aware of how others might feel on hearing it.

If you want to create a less heterosexist world (especially in your own home), be aware of what you say and how you say it. For example, instead of using terms like "boyfriend," "girlfriend," "husband," or "wife," try using the word "partner," which has no gender attached to it. Even using the word "homosexual" may be offensive to some—it sounds medical or clinical, like a disease, and suggests that homosexuality is, at best, about sex, and not about emotional connection or love. (I know, I know, you'll never please everybody, but is there any harm in being aware of how others may feel?)

We can create the next generation of tolerant and confident children. Recently my husband and I had dinner with friends and found ourselves discussing someone we knew who was married and still fighting his innate homosexuality for fear of parental rejection. This person was an adult, not a teen, but still felt the pressure to conform, even if it meant denying who he was. Around the table, we talked about the potential for all of us to be different kinds of parents—parents who were unconditionally supportive, protective, and accepting.

Isn't our role to nurture, love, and encourage our children to become independent, thoughtful, and happy members of society? In what way does sexual orientation preclude someone from being that? Hopefully we can all get past the old idea that "being gay is a choice" and start recognizing that "being gay is who we are."

Parents: How our kids treat others is a reflection of how we handle the issues of sexual orientation in our own homes. Encourage your children to treat people according to their character, and not whom they date or what they look like.

CHALLENGING THE STEREOTYPES

I am thankful that we finally live in a world where gay characters exist in our pop culture. Too often, however, gay characters are pretty stereotyped. When kids see these flamboyant gay men and "butch" lesbians in movies and television shows, they may believe that these characters represent gay individuals everywhere.

We have to explain that it is simply impossible to guess a person's orientation by the way they walk, or what they wear; the only way to know someone's sexual orientation is if he or she decides to share it with you.

Similarly, we have to challenge society's stereotypes of how men and women should behave. I was teaching in an all-boys school when one freshman said, "Homosexuality is weird." Naturally I asked why—not just out of curiosity, but because there was a good chance that someone in the class was gay, and if we don't challenge those statements, we implicitly say that they are correct.

The young man responded, "I don't know, lesbians are okay, but two men are weird. Girls can say they love each other or hold each other if they are crying, but I can't do that to another guy. It's just weird."

Weird or a sad commentary on male friendship? According to this student, lesbians were acceptable (and even "hot") because it's okay for women to show affection for one another, but gay men had to be weird. It was the first time I had heard this rationale: Gay men were strange not because they're sexually attracted to other men but because they're loving toward other men. Do men suppress their feelings with other males for fear of what may be said about them? Is this really the message we want to be sending to our sons? Or do we want them to know that we all need to let down our guards sometimes, and yes, there are times when we need a friend's shoulder to cry on.

How about incorporating some nontraditional books or films into your library? Let your kids know that there are all different types of families and relationships. Ever hear of *Heather Has Two Mommies*? It's an older book about nontraditional families, but there are many new young children's books, too: *Emma and Meesha My Boy: A Two Mom Story; The Duke Who Outlawed Jelly Beans and Other Stories; One Dad, Two Dads, Brown Dad, Blue Dads*. For teens, consider giving them *Am I Blue?: Coming Out from the Silence, Two Teenagers in Twenty: Writings by Gay and Lesbian Youth*, and *Not the Only One: Lesbian and Gay Fiction for Teens*.

DREAMS ARE NOT NECESSARILY REALITIES . . .
AND NEITHER IS A LITTLE EXPERIMENTATION

When I was in fourth grade, I had a dream that I was engaged in a passionate make-out session with Christie Brinkley. (I had probably just seen the *Sports Illustrated* swimsuit issue.) I awoke feeling nervous because I was sure my dream was not considered "normal." I wondered if it meant something was wrong with me. Well, sorry, Dr. Freud, but it was just a dream, and most of us have a same-sex dream at some time or another.

Not surprisingly, childhood is a time of intense and ever-changing feelings. Seemingly overnight, the opposite sex goes from having cooties to being hot. At the same time, same-sex friendship and same-sex love is common and has nothing to do with one's sexual orientation. Your child may ask you, "If I love [name of best friend], does that mean I'm gay?"

Explain that loving a friend is normal and that the feelings he or she has are perfectly natural—and don't prove anything one way or another about being gay. We love many people in our lives, but sexual orientation is about sexual attraction. To younger kids you might explain that when we talk about being gay we are talking about different kinds of feelings—like how Mommy and Daddy (or Mommy and Mommy or Daddy and Daddy) love each other and want to spend their lives together. Tell them that you know how they feel—that you love [insert your closest friend's name] the same way they love their friend. Hopefully, they will understand the comparison. If not, that's okay, too. It is a complicated issue and one they will have lots of questions about over the years. As long as you are willing to talk to them about these issues, you're in great shape.

Of course, there is a chance that your child's feelings for a friend *are* romantic. Don't freak out and don't jump to conclusions about your child's orientation. As I mentioned before, in childhood and adolescence, same-sex play is fairly common and typically represents mere curiosity. And when teens are curious, some find their closest friends of the same sex emotionally safe sexual partners. If they ask, explain that over time they will figure out who they are. They do not have to decide today.

"MOMMY, WHAT'S A TRANSVESTITE?"

Do you want to feel old? A class of eighth-graders asked me what a drag queen was. In my answer I made a reference to RuPaul. They looked at me blankly. How could they never have heard of her? She was a *huge* pop culture icon in the early nineties—oops, before they were born! Thankfully now, since the DVD release of *Rent*, I can point to the character of Angel if I'm trying to explain what a drag queen is. A drag queen is a man who performs or entertains dressed up as a woman.

It's easy to get confused about the concept of gender, but it's important to understand that gender is unrelated to sexual orientation. What gender you are (or want to be) does not determine what gender you are attracted to sexually. It gets even more complicated when we realize that it's possible for someone to be born looking like one gender but feeling like the other.

I often ask my younger classes to tell me how they know if someone is a man or woman. They run through a list of possibilities (hair, makeup, their name, their clothes, and so on), only to conclude that those attributes are not a definitive proof of gender. At some point, a kid will bite the bullet and say, "their genitals," but here's where the plot thickens. Yes, genitals are one of the main markers of gender, but it's not the whole story. Gender is made up of more than just genitals. There are men and women whose biological gender (their genitals) does not match their gender identity (what gender a person believes he or she is). When I explain this, kids typically react in hysteria or horror, depending on the class. But while it is easy to dismiss something so confusing and strange, don't. Even kids who will never struggle with an extreme type of gender dysmorphia will experience many gender-related issues, including whether they fit into the traditional expectations of masculinity or femininity. And let's be honest here—most of us don't fit perfectly; we are individuals.

One thing almost all kids will ask is if being a tomboy means that a girl wants to be a boy. The answer is no; what we wear and what activities we enjoy are just how we express ourselves. And that goes for boys as well. Just because your son likes dolls or playing in the kitchen doesn't mean he is gay. (So many boys are curious about "feminine" things that there is a children's book, called *Oliver Button Is a Sissy*, to help kids cope with the pressures of stereotypical gender roles.) But it is important to recognize that in our society a girl who "acts like a boy" is accepted; a boy who "acts like a girl" is not. These examples of gender roles are merely stereotypes of masculinity and femininity. They are not powerful enough to stand on their own. We should let our children express themselves any way they see fit.

There are other implications of labeling people and defining them by their gender and/or orientation. A teenage girl approached me after a class to find out who she was. (Yes, that's what I said, *who she was.*) "Logan, if I like girly, effeminate boys, what does that make me?"

She was trying to find out what category her particular sexual attractions put her in. Teens are desperate to determine if they are part of a crowd, or if they are destined to be alone because of their particular sexual proclivity. While I understand this student's need for information, it is upsetting to think that she felt the need to define herself with a word or group, rather than recognize that sexuality is fluid—and that we don't need the labels. Which is why I told her, "That's just who you are attracted to. You may always like feminine boys, or that may change. But don't worry about the label, it's just not important." She was appreciative that I didn't judge her or question her choices.

In the end, teens fear judgment, and sometimes the label justifies their choices because it makes them feel like "part of something." But perhaps we should do a better job at encouraging our teens to feel secure with their decisions so that they don't have to worry about the "group."

Unfortunately there is pressure to conform, and if you are unsure of who you are, the media's portrayal of gender issues doesn't help. Often the media link sexual orientation and gender together, satirizing them, or making them seem twisted and evil. (Think of all the cross-dressing or transgender murderers you see in the movies or on television dramas.)

The fact is that gender can be expressed in different ways. These labels are tossed around as if they are synonymous, but in actuality the definitions are quite unique.

Cross-dressers (or transvestites): People who (sexually) enjoy dressing in the clothes of the other gender. Transvestites don't want to be the other gender, but their sexuality does involve dressing as the other gender. Note that cross-dressers may be gay or straight; cross-dressing is not linked to homosexuality. In fact, transvestites are often heterosexual men who become aroused by wearing women's clothing.

Drag queen: Typically, a man who performs or entertains dressed up like a woman. They are commonly over-the-top and flamboyantly attired.

Drag king: a woman who performs in men's clothing, women who are aroused by dressing as a man, or women who wish to pass as a man. (But again, as women dressing in male clothing are seen as more acceptable, this term isn't used as frequently as "drag queen.")

Transgender: a person whose gender identity is different from his or her assigned (biological) gender. A transgendered person will often live as the other gender and may or may not seek to alter themselves surgically.

Transsexual: Similar to *transgender*, but a transsexual typically seeks surgical alteration.

WHAT IF MY KID IS GAY OR QUESTIONING HIS ORIENTATION?

What if your kid is gay? I would like to answer, "So what if he is?" but I know that would be inadequate. If you find that your child is starting to question his or her sexual orientation, it would be best to get *your* values in check first. Sometimes we need to identify how we really feel before we talk to our kids. We don't want to inadvertently send an unsupportive message.

It can be an emotionally challenging time for parents who realize that their children are not heterosexual, simply because our culture has not fully welcomed nonstraight persons wholeheartedly into the fold. And if we love our children, we want them to be accepted unconditionally. But the range of feelings that we have sometimes clouds our ability to think clearly. Most people speak of grief and mourning, as if they have lost a loved one during this "coming out" process. It is natural, and it will pass. What we hope is that these turbulent and complex feelings will bring you, in the end, to acceptance. But it isn't an easy road and I am not going to pretend that I have been through it. For these reasons, at the end of this book, you can find many wonderful resources for parents, LGBT (lesbian, gay, bisexual, transgender) youth, and parents who are LGBT themselves. These resources can provide you with information, support, and guidance, wherever you are in the world.

10 Common Questions About Gender and Sexual Orientation

1. DO GAY MEN WANT TO BE WOMEN? DO LESBIANS REALLY WANT TO BE MEN?

Sexual orientation refers to the gender of whom you are attracted to. It has nothing to do with what gender you want to be. Gay men and women are simply attracted to their own gender.

2. **WHAT IS IT CALLED IF SOMEONE HAS TWO MOMMIES (OR TWO DADDIES)?**

   It's called a family. I would use this as an opportunity to talk about the many different types of families there are in the world. Not every family looks or acts the same, but they are all based on one thing—love.

3. **HOW DO GAY PEOPLE HAVE SEX?**

   How you answer this question depends on how old your child is. You might not want to get into a conversation about nonvaginal intercourse. Simply explain that sex is just one way that adults express love for one another. Ask how else people show love (for example, hugging, kissing, touching). Gay people can do all of those things, too. Now, if your child is older and looking for more explicit information, you can talk to them about oral and anal sex. But keep in mind, not every gay couple engages in these activities and some heterosexual couples do.

4. **WHAT MAKES SOMEONE GAY?**

   No one knows for sure if sexual orientation is genetic or biological. What it isn't, is a choice; it is part of who we are. Adolescence is a time when many people begin to explore same-sex attractions and feelings, but others don't recognize their sexual orientation until they become adults. It is important to point out that many people experiment with people of the same sex during childhood and adolescence, so that is not a predictor of a person's orientation. It may simply be part of the learning process.

5. **WHAT DO I DO IF I THINK THAT I AM GAY?**

   If children or teens are asking this, it is important to tell them that they are not alone. There are millions of people who have the same feelings. If they are questioning their orientation, they should try to find someone they trust to talk to. This may be a parent, a relative, a friend, or some other person who they can confide in. There are many resources available to them to help them share some of their thoughts and hear the stories of others who have already gone through what they are experiencing. (Some of these resources are listed at the end of this book.)

6. WOULD YOU BE DISAPPOINTED IN ME IF I WAS GAY?

Many of us look for our parents' approval. If your child is questioning his orientation he may be asking this to gauge your response and level of support. If you find yourself in this situation, make sure you tell your child that you love him no matter what. Ask him what he needs from you and try to give that to him. If you have questions or concerns of your own, which is perfectly normal, get some assistance. PFLAG (Parents, Families and Friends of Lesbians and Gays) is a parents' group devoted to helping parents and their children deal with issues of sexual orientation.

7. WHY ARE SOME PEOPLE HOMOPHOBIC?

Some people are uncomfortable around anyone who is different from themselves, especially if sexual orientation is something that they just don't understand. What we need to realize is that sexual orientation is simply another part of our identity, just like our gender, race, or religion. We need to be tolerant of all people regardless of who they are sexually attracted to.

8. HOW MANY PEOPLE ARE GAY OR LESBIAN?

We don't have good statistics. Consider why this may be so:
(1) Some people do not want to respond to surveys about homosexuality; (2) The answer may depend on what area of the country

is being surveyed—small towns, big cities, and so on; (3) Some
people who have same-sex behaviors may not identify as gay or
lesbian. The estimate that Kinsey proposed during his work in the
late 1940s was 10 percent of the population, and a 2000 U.S.
Census report suggests that it is 5 percent. But even if we don't
know exact numbers, we do know that there is a rich gay culture in
this world.

9. **DO GAY PEOPLE WANT TO TURN YOU GAY?**

Homosexuality isn't a cult and gay people aren't looking to "turn"
you away from being heterosexual. What gay people *do* want is to
be accepted like anyone else.

10. **HOW DO YOU DEAL WITH A GAY FRIEND?**

Deal with a gay friend the same way you deal with a straight friend.
Just because a friend has told you he's gay doesn't mean that he has
changed. Treat him with the same respect and care that you did
before you knew his sexual orientation and be there for him if he
needs your support. "Coming out" is a big event, and you should
feel proud that your friend trusted you enough to tell you.

Chapter Six

SEX: ORAL, ANAL, VAGINAL, AND NONE AT ALL

While we can barely go five minutes without hearing the word "sex," how do we know we're all talking about the same thing? Twenty years ago you could get an answer to the question "Did you have sex?" and know what that meant with relative certainty. Not now. Because sex isn't necessarily "sex" anymore. It's old news that former president Clinton did not consider blow jobs to be sex, but I'm not sure that any of us could have foreseen oral sex becoming a behavior so pervasively trivialized. To those of us who are not part of today's teen population, it can be shocking that something so intimate can be taken so lightly.

In the spring of 2000, when newspapers and magazines first began to investigate these "popular" sexual behaviors, I was conducting an investigation of my own. During an eighth-grade workshop, I posed the following question to forty girls: "How is oral sex different from sexual intercourse?" As if they had been thinking about this question for weeks, four hands quickly shot up. One after another, the girls gave their answers:

"Sexual intercourse is far more intimate. Oral sex is no big deal."

"Please, it's like we're doing them [the boys] a favor!"

"It's not like we even look at their faces."

"C'mon, it's, like, third base!"

What a switch. When I was in high school it was far more acceptable to have sexual intercourse than to have oral sex. Though today's teens are surprised that generations past didn't embrace oral sex as the "no big deal" behavior of their youth, it is important that they hear our stories. In addition to giving them a peek into our minds, it gives teens the opportunity to critically examine why their world is so different.

Vicky (not her real name) was in my tenth-grade gym class. We were in the girls' locker room when we overheard her whispering to a friend that she had given a blow job to someone. Within moments, the entire gym class (and from there, the entire grade and school) had learned what Vicky had done. To use the term "social pariah" would be an understatement. Because even if Vicky had never come close to a penis, once the blow job rumor was out there, it was impossible to get it back. She was forever branded a slut.

Now the fact that I remember this goes to show you how powerful the label was. But more important, it illustrates the difference between then and now. Poor Vicky might have had oral sex under ideal circumstances—with a partner she loved and trusted, who respected her and himself, and using protection. But we never knew that. All we knew was that she was willing to put her mouth on some guy's penis. Where I grew up, this was an unforgivable sin.

Why was oral sex so taboo? First, simply because it seemed disgusting to put your mouth *there*. Second, we didn't like the image of a girl being "on her knees," subservient to a boy. Third, because "good girls" didn't do it, we knew we'd be talked about in boys' locker rooms for years to come. (Of course, that was my experience with oral sex. Some of my friends and colleagues argue that the incidence of oral sex hasn't changed that much; it's the attitude about it that's changed.) Notice the negative beliefs embedded in that taboo: that genitals are dirty and shameful, when they're not. That giving oral sex means giving up control, which it doesn't. That oral sex is something women perform on men and not vice versa—a definite no!

So if in many ways our old attitudes about oral sex were so misguided, why not cheer for today's teens' discarding of them? Well, unfortunately their new attitudes are just as screwed up. Oral sex is no big deal, we're doing boys a favor, and we don't even need to look at them? It seems we haven't come far at all. The biggest problems with sexuality and adolescence remain lack of intimacy, lack of pleasure, and lack of self-esteem. The girls' statements also explain why oral sex has become popular: (1) You maintain the title of "virgin" while participating in explicit sexual behaviors, and (2) performing fellatio ("blow jobs") is an easy way to keep boyfriends appeased without having intercourse.

When I asked these girls if they were ever the recipients of oral sex, I was confronted with faces of disgust and horror. They seemed mortified by the suggestion. (I believe they answered, "Ugh. Down there? That's so gross!") Herein lies the problem. We are raising a new generation of women who are set up to be mere performers in their sexual encounters.

Time and again I'm dismayed by how girls perceive their innate sexuality and their own bodies. While they are quick to discuss blow jobs, they blush at the idea of masturbation; they consider pleasing a partner their "job" yet refuse to believe that their own bodies deserve pleasure as well. We should all be concerned about how this perception, combined with the actual sexual experimentation, creates an environment where young women wind up unfulfilled, physically and emotionally.

Most of the time oral sex is a one-sided activity. Boys aren't expected to reciprocate. Boys don't always want to reciprocate. And girls are still "servicing." Many adult men jokingly say to me, "Where were all of these girls when I was their age?" And it's easy to see why they ask. What guy is going to turn down a relationship-free, no-ties blow job? (Can you imagine the taunts he would hear if word got around that he refused?) But for those of us with sons, how are we to respond? They need to know about reciprocation, about respecting partners, and about the health risks that come from unprotected oral sex. We want to teach our sons how to be men—real men—who know the pleasure that comes from both giving and receiving.

The girls need the same lessons as the boys. The old excuses about having sex "to keep a boyfriend" or "to get someone to like you" still exist. And it is not as if the girls don't know better. They admit that these are poor reasons for engaging in any kind of sex behavior, but they "can't help" themselves. Sometimes the pressures of being a teen, and wanting to be close to someone, override higher decision making. I fear that we don't encourage our daughters to embrace their sexuality in healthy ways. And if we don't start giving honest information to our girls, then we are bound to create a generation of sexual Stepford wives—girls who perform and please without demanding anything in return.

In a surprising turn of events, some girls have told me that they perform oral sex because it puts them in control. A teenage girl announced in class one day, "If I am giving a blow job, I have the power. He can't have pleasure without me." While it is an interesting argument, I fear that for most teenage girls, this is a tremendous fallacy. Girls who think that their bodies are repulsive are unlikely to feel powerful from giving blow jobs. If these were girls who were demanding pleasure in return and not compromising themselves for the sake of others, I might believe otherwise. But for now, I am definitely not convinced.

What is it in this world that makes women frightened to accept their own sexual drives? Is it the fear of being branded a slut or is it years of listening to boys brag about their sexual conquests? It is almost expected for boys to be "players"; girls are left to pick up the pieces of their shattered reputations. In addition to the general teen rumor mill, girls may deny their sexual feelings because they are trying to avoid the humiliation of having intimate and personal details about their performance and their bodies described in a public high school forum.

When you talk about oral sex, make sure to mention protection. By always including condoms in your discussions, your kids won't ever consider having oral sex without one.

I have always had a feeling that oral sex became popular because we never thought to talk about it. Even when AIDS made us much more open, as a society, to talking about sex, we focused on vaginal intercourse and anal sex as if they were the only important concerns. We were very wrong, and our omission implicitly told teens that oral sex was an acceptable behavior. Acceptable, because if we didn't talk about it, it must be okay. Yes, it is very possible that the prevalence of oral sex among teens is actually our fault. But whatever the reason, it is our responsibility to provide our children with accurate information regarding oral sex (and, of course, sexuality as a whole). Let's face facts: Oral sex is now part of the social fabric, and we need to decide how to educate our teens. They are still under the impression that oral sex is risk-free sex. We need to spread the word that oral sex does put you at risk for sexually transmitted diseases (though the degree of risk is different for each STD). And if they or their friends are going to engage in these behaviors, then they have to know about protection. But this only works if we are allowed and empowered to talk about it.

ABSTINENCE: DOES IT WORK?

Politicians are constantly talking about "abstinence only until marriage" sex education. Now don't get me wrong, abstinence isn't bad—in fact, abstinence is the best option for many teens. But it isn't the only option, and for some parents that's a hard thing to admit. The fact is, abstinence may not be as safe as we think. I know, parents all over the country are shaking their heads right now. What do you mean, abstinence isn't safe? Isn't abstinence the only safe thing out there? Actually, abstinence is tricky, far more so than its proponents are willing to tell you.

But before we tackle that tricky point, let's define the *a*-word clearly: Abstinence is refraining from any behavior that could put someone at risk for sexually transmitted diseases, pregnancy, and/ or HIV/AIDS. That means vaginal intercourse, oral sex, or anal sex. While this may seem fairly obvious to you, many kids do not share this definition. For many of them, abstinence refers solely to sexual intercourse and not other potentially risky sexual behaviors. So the first problem with lecturing about abstinence is that your teen might think he's agreeing to something quite different. When parents assume that their children are on the same page with them, especially with respect to abstinence, they may stop having conversations about sex because they have concluded that their teen has committed to abstaining from all types of sexual behaviors. If this is the case, we miss the boat entirely.

Parents aren't necessarily to blame. There is great miscommunication surrounding abstinence, and parents and schools are sometimes bullied into thinking that abstinence-only works. But abstinence-only sexual education is greatly flawed. The Society for Adolescent Medicine released a report stating that abstinence-only education "is ethically problematic, as it excludes accurate information about contraception, misinforms by overemphasizing or misstating the risks of contraception, and fails to require the use of scientifically accurate information while promoting approaches of questionable value" (Santelli, Ott, Lyon, Rogers, Summers & Schleifer, 2006). U.S. Representative Henry Waxman of California in his 2004 report on current abstinence-only curricula also found that the information present in popular programs is misleading and inaccurate, and perpetuates old gender stereotypes (Waxman, 2004). In addition, there has been no good evidence to suggest that abstinence-only programs are successful in delaying the onset of sexual behavior; research has concluded this, time and time again (Kirby, 2000; Satcher, 2001).* But more than one billion dollars ($141 million in 2007) have been funneled into these educational interventions in a fruitless attempt to curb adolescent sexuality (not just sex) altogether. While abstinence can be an appropriate choice for teens, the information in abstinence-only education does not provide students with the tools necessary to have a happy and healthy life.

Most parents don't even understand what abstinence-only programs teach. According to Title V of the Social Security Act, Section 510b, "abstinence only until marriage" education means an educational or motivational program that:

1. has as its exclusive purpose teaching the social, psychological, and health gains to be realized by abstaining from sexual activity;
2. teaches abstinence from sexual activity outside marriage as the expected standard for all school-age children;
3. teaches that abstinence from sexual activity is the only certain way to avoid out-of-wedlock pregnancy, sexually transmitted diseases, and other associated health problems;
4. teaches that a mutually faithful monogamous relationship in the context of marriage is the expected standard of sexual activity;

* On April 13, 2007, a federally funded ten-year evaluation of abstinence-only programs was released. It was found that abstinence-only programs had no impact on adolescent behavior. (http://www.mathematica=mpr.com/publications/PDFs/impactabstinence)

5. teaches that sexual activity outside of the context of marriage is likely to have harmful psychological and physical effects;

6. teaches that bearing children out of wedlock is likely to have harmful consequences for the child, the child's parents, and society;

7. teaches young people how to reject sexual advances and how alcohol and drug use increase vulnerability to sexual advances; and

8. teaches the importance of attaining self-sufficiency before engaging in sexual activity.

What happens to the teens who may already be sexually active, were sexually abused, or don't come from a traditional two-parent family? Are they included in this discussion or forced to sit in silence or disgrace? Are you prepared to defend the idea that all sexual activity outside of marriage, which would include masturbation, has "harmful psychological and physical effects," even between consenting adults? Even compared to an abusive marriage? And if that weren't enough, Title V explicitly forbids the discussion of contraceptive methods and other safer sex options, further creating a culture of guilt, shame, and ignorance.

In 2006, a new funding announcement by the Department of Health and Human Services for community-based abstinence education (CBAE) programs laid out more than just the eight points of Title V. Newly required topics include, but are certainly not limited to: the failure of contraceptive methods; that having premarital sex can be viewed as a character flaw and a significant lack of integrity; that premarital sex leads to lower school completion rates; that sexual desires can be controlled; and that the "expected standard" for relationships is between a man and a woman (SIECUS, 2006). These programs assume that the world is heterosexual, that everyone should be married, and that unless you are married, sex is deadly and reflects poorly on you. Abstinence-only programs lie to children both by providing misinformation and by omission (Santelli, et al., 2006).

But what good does that do, anyway? Teens are already suspicious of our motives when we talk about sex. After the second session of one seventh-grade program, I asked the kids if they were surprised by anything we had spoken about in our first class. A girl raised her hand and said, "I was surprised that you were so positive about sex. I expected you to come in here and say, Don't have sex, you'll die." That's exactly what we don't want kids to think. Scare tactics don't work—they simply shut down the conversation.

The fact is, 55 percent of teens between the ages of fifteen and seventeen have been sexually and physically intimate with another person, including but not limited to vaginal intercourse (Hoff, 2003). It is unreasonable to think that you are going to get everyone to stop cold turkey. It's just not possible, and teen sexuality is not always bad. What *is* bad is not giving teens the whole story.

I am not anti-abstinence. I am, however, against the assumptions that abstinence is the right choice for everyone and that abstinence-only education is a panacea. Perhaps my biggest complaint is that abstinence is not held to the same standards and rigorous testing as other contraceptive methods. Yes, if abstinence is practiced perfectly, and practiced every time, then it is 100 percent effective. Rarely do people practice abstinence this way, however. At some point in their lives, teens decide to be sexually active; not all of them wait until they are married—not even the teens who take a virginity pledge. There is a failure rate of abstinence, whether we want to believe it or not (Dailard, 2003).

There has been a wave of abstinence movements in this country. There is a population actively pursuing mass adolescent chastity through virginity pledges, commitment ceremonies, like "the Silver Ring Thing" (SRT), and father-daughter purity balls. SRT is a ceremony where teens make a public vow of abstinence as a commitment to God. As a sign of their pledge, they wear a silver ring, which is to be removed upon their wedding. And if that weren't enough, purity balls call for a father to be his daughter's sexual keeper. After waltzing around a ballroom the daughters make a virginity pledge, not to God but to their fathers. The fathers in turn pledge to protect them, and also to act purely (though they can still have sex). The idea of sexualizing the father-daughter relationship is not only creepy, but scares fathers away from actually engaging in their daughters' lives. And how come there are no purity balls for mothers and sons? It appears that the abstinence movement believes in a sexual double standard that boys "don't need" parental guidance in their sex lives, which as you well know is ridiculous for many reasons.

Regardless, CBAE programs and virginity pledges have been found to be ineffective. According to a study presented at the National STD Prevention Conference in 2004 (Bearman and Bruckner), teens who pledge virginity have similar rates of STD infection to those who do not pledge. Part of this is due to the lack of contraceptive use by pledgers and lack of STD testing. In essence, these fearmongering abstinence programs just don't work, because teens are humans, and we all have certain desires that can't always be suppressed, no matter how hard we try.

A WORD ABOUT VIRGINITY

Though we can presumably all agree that thirteen-year-olds should not be having sexual intercourse or any other form of sex, the concept of virginity quickly grows more complicated. A relentless focus on maintaining virginity pressures teens to deny or repress their natural desires, forcing them to find other ways to "act out." Some teens engage in oral and anal sex because they are not perceived as means of losing one's virginity. Second, the burden of maintaining virginity is often unfairly left to girls, as though they have greater responsibilities and face greater consequences than their male partners. Boys should take sex as seriously as girls do. It is not only a physical behavior but an emotional one as well. When we leave girls with the task of protecting their chastity, it sets boys and girls up to have unequal relationships, where one person is trying to "score" and the other is trying to fight off her partner's advances. A healthy relationship is one where both partners are responsible for safety and respectful of each other's decisions. We want our sons to become men who don't shirk their responsibilities. Boys will never learn how to become decent, responsible men, however, if we continue to perpetuate the idea that girls need more protection than they do. Last, we should all be aware that virginity as commonly understood is a heterosexist concept. Have you ever considered what happens to boys and girls who aren't interested in vaginal intercourse? If they never participate in penile-vaginal sex, are they virgins forever? I don't expect that any of us have an answer to this, but it is a great philosophical question to pose to your teen. If anything, it gets all of us thinking about what virginity really is.

> **D**on't forget that the best conversations go two ways. If your child asks you a question about sex, you can always use it as an opening to ask questions of them, too.

SHOULD PEOPLE REALLY WAIT UNTIL MARRIAGE?

Well, sex isn't always bad. In fact, don't the experiences we have growing up provide the foundation for who we are as adults? Some teen relationships are loving and respectful. And if a teen is going to have sex for the first time, I would rather see it within the context of this type of relationship than after getting drunk at a frat party, or worse, at the prom. Sexual chemistry is important in a relationship, and sex before marriage is not necessarily a bad idea. Now, this doesn't mean that children should be having sex; but there are some adolescents who are capable of making a sexual decision. And if we have done our job as parents, then these teens will make the right choice for themselves.

After all, a healthy relationship includes good sex, which is not necessarily a given if one or both partners hasn't had any prior experience. My parents (my father especially) always told my sister and me that sexuality was a special and vital part of our lives and that whenever we decided to have sex it should be on our own terms: because we wanted it, not at someone else's urging, and because we knew how—and were going—to be safe. Those words were empowering and allowed us to feel confident about the decisions we were one day going to make. And while you may think that my parents' attitudes may have sped up my adolescent experimentation with sexual intercourse, it actually did just the opposite. Because I knew how wonderful and important sex was, I waited until the right relationship came along, which wound up being long after most of my friends had sex for the first time. Just because you acknowledge the importance of sex doesn't mean that you encourage your children to have it. But we should examine what we really want for our children. Is it that we want them all to wait until marriage, or that we want them to avoid the negative aspects of sexuality—unintended pregnancy, sexually transmitted diseases, and emotional abuse? Though we don't always like to admit it, it is possible to avoid these things and enjoy sex, even during adolescence.

Let's face it: If you don't give children any information about contraception and safer sex, then they don't develop the skills or knowledge to become sexually healthy beings—whether they save themselves for marriage or not.* You can encourage abstinence while simultaneously giving children the tools to one day make informed decisions about sex.

Perhaps the biggest challenge to talking to our children about sexuality is that most of us have a hidden agenda. We want to be honest, but we don't want to encourage them to go out and actually do it. One of the ways we may handle that conflict is to conveniently forget to tell them about pleasure. You may fear that if you tell your children about orgasms, they will head right out to look for them. In actuality, our children already know that sex is pleasurable, otherwise people wouldn't be doing it. And if they have any doubt, expo-

---

* Though most Americans are not saving themselves at all. A 2007 study (Finer, 2007) found that nine out of ten people do engage in premarital sex.

sure to any given day's advertising, TV, movies, or music will put it to rest. So if you minimize or ignore sexual pleasure, they will think that you are lying to them, and ignore everything else that you say (even if it looks like they are listening).

An exercise we often do in my classes is brainstorm reasons why someone might decide to have sex or not have sex. One sixth-grade boy said pleasure should be on the first list. I told him that he was right. Pleasure is absolutely a reason. Other suggestions followed: they are old enough, they are in love, they know about safe sex, they want to have a baby, and so on. Another boy raised his hand and offered, "It feels good." I said, yes, we can include that under "pleasure." Well, the first boy looked quizzical. "What do you mean it feels good? I meant you are in love so you get pleasure from loving someone." He had no idea that pleasure could refer to physical pleasure. And I had assumed that's what he was talking about, which goes to show how important it is that we ask our kids to define everything that they say. What do they really mean? Chances are their definitions will change how and what we say to them.

Discussing sexual pleasure is complicated also because it forces us to consider our own sexuality. Do we demand pleasure in our own lives? And what do we actually want for our children? Do we want them to have pleasureless encounters or do we want them to grow up to have fulfilling sexual experiences? If we teach them about pleasure, and explain to them that they can access it on their own—yes, by masturbating—then they won't need to seek out pleasure from a partner.

Human sexuality isn't simply about an instinctual drive to mate. Humans need emotional connection and psychological satisfaction as well. Our sexuality is not limited to physical sensation. Our minds and our emotions are a huge piece of the puzzle. This idea is often lost on teens because their hormones trick them into thinking sex is merely physical, but it is impossible to be sexually satisfied if our minds remain unsatisfied. This dissatisfaction can be due to lack of protection, poor body image, anxiety about performance, and even second-guessing your decision. We tend to forget that our minds control much of how we respond sexually.

> Teens often tell me, "Using a condom doesn't feel as good as natural skin-to-skin contact." Now, the funny part is that most boys who claim this have never had condomless sex (if any sex at all). They're simply making assumptions based on what they hear others saying. My response is that if you are constantly wondering, "Is this going to be the time when I get an STD or pregnant?" then unprotected sex is definitely not going to feel good. Our brain just gets in the way. And we should be thankful for that, because it allows us to make better decisions.

Body image is a huge contributor to dissatisfaction. Our self-esteem and self-image greatly affect how we express ourselves sexually. Some people simply perform and pleasure others, and for others, their awareness of their own desires allows them to create balanced relationships, where reciprocation is essential. These equal relationships are what we should be modeling for our children, and if that isn't available to us, we should be teaching them the importance of reciprocation. But feeling good about how we look (and yes, sometimes what we weigh) also affects how engaged we are in our relationships. Think about how hard it is to show your naked body to someone if you can't stand what you see in the mirror. You are more likely to suppress your own needs in an effort to conceal who you are and what you look like. In a good relationship (the ones we want to teach our children about), partners don't make us feel guilty about our flaws; they love us with them. Moreover, no one wants a partner who is so consumed by negative body image that she cannot enjoy physical intimacy. And if we cannot show ourselves to someone else, are we are ready for involvement in a sexual relationship?

LOOKING FOR "SAFE" EXPERIMENTATION? TRY IT WITH A FRIEND

I was totally kidding. But it is the rationale behind a commonly discussed relationship. In an effort to experiment with supposed emotional safety, many teens are trying out a relationship commonly called "friends with benefits" (FWB). The idea is that these couplings are based upon platonic friendships but have the privilege of sexual experimentation. While you might have had one of your own when you were a teen, it was hardly a movement large enough to warrant a title. I, for one, have very serious concerns about the ramifications of these types of relationships, and not because I think that sex needs to be within the confines of a larger romance. Rather, I fear that with teens who are just beginning to understand their sexuality, these relationships are not emotionally safe. Inevitably someone gets hurt. If your teen happens to talk about these "casual" relationships, you might want to put some things into perspective for them, because many teens see these as ideal relationships—you know, all of the experimentation with none of the guilt.

Let us not forget that while it is completely natural to want to experiment, it is also in our nature (it is at least stereotypical for females) to become emotionally attached. What begins as a playful, safe sexual relationship sometimes evolves into a one-sided love affair. I am not so pompous as to suggest that this is true for all FWB, but it is common, and that shouldn't come as a surprise. It is far easier to create a sexual relationship with someone you like under the guise of it being FWB than it is to be emotionally vulnerable and put your feelings out there to be embraced or crushed. So as this relationship develops, even with no technical strings attached, someone begins to fall into love (or into what seems like love). The nature of friendships during adolescence is so fragile to begin with. Sex can create a larger problem . . . and in some cases, friendships may end altogether. If that weren't enough to make someone think more clearly about an FWB relationship, teens gossip. There is no guarantee that their encounters will be kept confidential. If someone isn't comfortable with other people knowing their business, this may not be the best relationship to be involved in.

What is wrong with intimacy? It appears that teens have no idea what it means, and we should be explaining that intimacy can be both physical and emotional and it isn't something we should run from. It can be a wonderful, if not necessary, component of a relationship.

On the other side, though teens may not be sharing their feelings in these relationships, there may be an underlying benefit to FWB with respect to sexual communication. The obvious benefit from this type of coupling is that teens can practice talking about their sexual past, because chances are their "friend" already knows about it. Friends know who we sleep with, how often, and (maybe) whether or not we've had an STD because of it. Because they are just "friends," however, there is a chance that their partner is sleeping with other people and it is crucial that they still protect themselves.

As a parent, I think that if a teen is going to experiment, I would want them to do so with someone who cares about them and protects them physically and emotionally. Parents need to be up front with their children and explain this to them. It's not that you want to lock them up forever; you just want to make sure they have the best that life has to offer, without getting hurt. You can help teens examine the pros and cons of FWB, even if it is in the context of talking about a relationship that "their friend" is having. But you can decide for yourself: Are FWB platonic, romantic, or mislabeled?

THE FIVE BIGGEST SEX MYTHS

Whether your teens are dating, FWB, or abstinent, they are still affected by some old sexual myths. And these myths—if bought into—can mean the difference between a healthy sexual life and contracting a sexually transmitted disease or getting pregnant.

1. A WOMAN CANNOT BECOME PREGNANT IF SHE HAS UNPROTECTED SEX DURING HER PERIOD.

Everyone is shocked to hear that this is a myth. Yes, you're much less likely to become pregnant during menstruation, but it is technically possible. And the slight chance isn't worth the risk of participating in unprotected sex.

2. **ORAL SEX IS SAFE SEX.**

   Though oral sex is the least common means of HIV transmission, it definitely comes with risks. Other sexually transmitted diseases can be spread through oral sex, both protected and unprotected.

3. **"PULLING OUT" IS AN EFFECTIVE SAFER-SEX METHOD FOR TEENS.**

   "Pulling out," or withdrawal, is definitely not an effective method of safer sex. First, men produce preejaculatory fluid (commonly called "precum"). This fluid comes out of the penis before a man ejaculates and may contain sperm. So even if the man withdraws his penis before his climax, it is possible to get pregnant, and definitely still possible to contract an STD if he has one. Pulling out is also problematic because you need to rely on your partner to know exactly when he is going to ejaculate . . . and there is no guarantee that is going to happen.

4. **IF A PERSON LOOKS "CLEAN," HE OR SHE IS "CLEAN."**

   This myth is perpetuated today simply because the old scare tactics of our youth are still utilized by some educators and parents. Did your science teacher show you pictures of cauliflower-like masses growing on penises and around vulvas in an effort to scare you away from sex? (We saw those pictures in my classes and swore to be abstinent forever.) Kids see the same images today and assume that when a person has an STD it is easily identifiable. Unfortunately, most STDs have few or no symptoms (unless an illness has progressed without intervention). So if a person looks "clean" there is still no guarantee that he doesn't have some sexually transmitted disease. The fear-based strategy completely backfires.

5. **ANAL AND ORAL SEX ARE GOOD WAYS OF MAINTAINING YOUR VIRGINITY.**

I would hardly consider anal and oral sex as behaviors that help to maintain virginity. Just because someone hasn't engaged in vaginal intercourse doesn't mean that he is still "chaste." In an effort to stay virgins, people participate in other sex behaviors because they don't carry the same weight (in their minds) as intercourse. But the risks are still there. They don't go away just because you are still a "virgin."

Be clear with your children. If you tell them that they should be abstinent, explain what you mean by that and give them your reasons. If you make a blanket statement without backing it up, teens are less likely to buy into it.

OKAY, SO HOW WILL I KNOW WHEN I'M READY?

Your kids will ask you this question at some point, and though it is not an easy conversation to have, it is a necessary one. You're entitled to share your feelings with your children—especially your feelings about sex. If you don't think that they are ready for the responsibilities that come with being sexually active, tell them. But know that they may ask you why you question their judgment. And if they do that, you are going to need to give them honest answers—or at least give them some criteria to help them make what will inevitably be their decision, not yours.

The reasons below cover only some of the issues that are important when deciding whether to have sex, but are often left unspoken. We are quick to say, "You're too young," "You're not responsible," or "You're not really in love," but those don't resonate with teens. Those may reflect a parent's concerns, but they are disconnected from what your kids are feeling and experiencing. So here are criteria that may help you through a difficult conversation about readiness. Feel free to add or edit as you see fit—you know your child best.

You may not be ready to have sex if . . .

- You are unaware of the outcomes of sexual activity (positive and negative)
- You are uncomfortable talking about safer sex or a partner's sexual history
- You are too embarrassed to purchase a box of condoms or another form of safe sex/contraception
- You are unwilling to see a doctor as soon as you become sexually active

> **A**ssure your teens that their sexual feelings are normal, but ask them to talk to you before they decide to be sexually active.

GIVING YOUR KIDS CONDOMS:
IS IT THE EASY WAY OUT?

Some parents are quick to throw a box of Trojans at their teens in an effort to be enlightened and helpful, but this strategy may be counterproductive. The summer before my senior year in high school, I went to a student program in Cambridge, Massachusetts. As my date of departure approached, visions of my upcoming social life danced through my mind. I was seventeen and sure that this was going to be the best summer of my life—and by that, I mean that I thought I would be having sex. I told my mom that I needed some condoms. While my mother was shocked (I didn't even have a boyfriend), she insisted that I go and buy them myself. She said, "Logan, if you are ready to consider having sex, then you have to be ready to buy your own condoms." And she wasn't giving me the money for them, either.

So one day after school, I put on big dark sunglasses and a baseball cap and headed to my hometown pharmacy. I got up to the counter with my Trojan blue pack, not realizing that my mom's closest friend was standing right behind me watching my entire transaction. (But there is a lesson in that, too: If you are ready for sex, then you should be ready to talk to your parents about it openly—though I am quite certain that this is the most difficult thing for a teen to do.)

In case you were wondering, I didn't use those condoms; turns out I wasn't ready to have sex after all. But my roommate did, so at least they were put to good use. Now, many years later and a parent myself, I commend my parents (I include my father because I am sure that he was in on the deal) for encouraging me to purchase my own sexual health supplies. They instilled in me the sense of sexual responsibility that I live with to this day. Often, parents become confused and think that by giving children condoms they are actually empowering them. But you should be providing them with solid sexual health information, not just condoms. We actually send teens the wrong message when we are the sole providers of prophylactics. In a sense we treat them as children, taking responsibility for their safety, even as we acknowledge that they are engaging in adult activities. It's very confusing. It's as if you are saying, "You are old enough to have sex, but not old enough to be responsible." If you don't encourage your children to take care of their own sexual health supplies, they may become dependent on your resources and may not be prepared when it really counts—when you are not around to slip a condom under their bedroom door. More important, sex is a responsibility, and in order to be sexually active, a teen should have to take care of his or her own sexual health. It goes with the territory. If you are going to use them, you need to buy them. And all teens should have them, just in case.

Okay, so with that being said, it isn't a bad idea to have condoms in your house, because part of adolescence unfortunately includes not planning ahead, and we don't want teens to have any excuses for not using condoms.

ANAL SEX

Now, I don't want to forget about anal sex, because if my earlier theory is accurate, the less we talk about it and its potential risks or benefits, the more kids are going to try it. Anal sex will probably never become as "trendy" as oral sex, simply because it involves a part of our anatomy that is used for excretion. Many people can't get past that. But we need to acknowledge that it does exist, people do it, it can be pleasurable, and it does come with risks. True, there is no risk of pregnancy, but unprotected anal sex is the riskiest behavior for contracting all sexually transmitted diseases. We need to know this, because our kids are going to ask about it. They will want to know what it is, why people do it, and whether it is something they would consider doing. The short answers to those three: (1) Anal sex is contact between the genitals and the anus (primarily the penis and the anus); (2) When it comes to sex, everyone is different—some people find it pleasurable; and (3) You may never try it, and that's fine, or there may come a time when you want to try it. One thing is certain—no one has to do anything that they don't want to. Hopefully these responses should do the trick. But you should also include a message about the sexual health risks posed by anal sex. This can be done as simply as: "Though you cannot become pregnant, anal sex is not considered safer sex and should never be done without a condom."

Teens tend to be fascinated by anal sex—not because they want to try it, but because they are curious about what kind of pleasure, if any, can come from it. The answer is simple: When a man receives anal sex, his prostate is stimulated. Most of us only know the prostate gland with respect to cancer, but when stimulated, it can cause sexual pleasure. Some people also feel sexual pleasure from the stimulation of the anus, which is why women may enjoy anal sex as well, even though they don't have prostates. As a whole, it is important to stress that every person's body is different; every person gets pleasure in different ways. When you speak about anal sex, try to be as judgment-free as possible. If our teens have tried anal sex, or are curious about trying it, we don't want them to feel guilty or ashamed. We want them to know all of the facts so that they can make educated decisions and protect themselves.

Tell your teens that sexual responsibility includes more than just using protection. They need to be tested, buy their own condoms, and communicate with their partners about sexual health. In order to really be "ready," teens need to be responsible for the pre- and postsexual event.

---

10 Common Questions About Sex Children and Teens Want Answers To

1. DOES A MAN ALWAYS EJACULATE THE SAME AMOUNT EVERY TIME?

The answer is no. Every ejaculation is different. (I was once asked this question by a girl who wrote: "I had sex with my boyfriend and afterward, he was scared. Looking at the condom, he said he didn't ejaculate his 'usual' amount. He examined the condom to see if there were holes in it. He didn't see any. But could I be pregnant?"

It's no surprise teens may be concerned about the consistency of ejaculations.)

2. **WHY DO MEN AND WOMEN HAVE ANAL SEX IF THEY CAN HAVE REGULAR SEX?**

What's regular sex? (When I get this kind of question I assume someone is talking about vaginal intercourse, but you never know. That's why you need to ask.) Explain that people are different and couples may decide to express themselves in many ways, including, but not limited to, vaginal intercourse. Also, some people have anal sex because it feels pleasurable to them.

3. **HOW DO YOU MAKE ORAL SEX SAFER?**

A man receiving oral sex (a blow job) should wear a latex condom, preferably without spermicide on it. If a condom is lubricated with spermicide, the chemicals can make your mouth numb. There are also flavored condoms that are designed for safer oral sex. A woman receiving oral sex (commonly called "going down") can protect herself and her partner by using a "dental dam," a square of latex that is placed on top of the vulva and vaginal opening so that there is no direct contact between the mouth and the genitals. Sometimes you can purchase dental dams at stores that sell male condoms, but they can be hard to find. Dental dams can be created from a condom, however. Cut off the tip, cut lengthwise down the condom, then unroll to form one large latex square. This square will be identical to a dental dam.

4. **CAN YOU GET PREGNANT FROM ANAL OR ORAL SEX?**

No. There is no risk of pregnancy from anal sex or oral sex. If anal sex is unprotected, however, and semen drips into the woman's vagina, there is always a chance of pregnancy.

5. FOR A WOMAN, HOW COME SEX HURTS THE FIRST TIME?

Some women (though not every one) experience pain and/or
bleeding the first time or first few times they have sex. Pain and
bleeding may be due to a number of issues, including tearing of the
hymen (though sometimes the hymen "breaks" long before a girl
has intercourse), stretching of the vagina, and vaginal dryness (poor
lubrication). In addition, if a woman is anxious about having sex and
cannot relax, she may find intercourse uncomfortable—a sign that
she may not be "ready."

6. CAN YOU HAVE SEX IF THE WOMAN IS HAVING HER PERIOD?

Women can definitely have sex when they're menstruating.

7. DO MOST PEOPLE SPIT OR SWALLOW?

Every person experiences sex differently, so we don't have an
answer for that. (Neither, by the way, is considered "safe" from an
STD perspective.)

8. HOW LONG DO PEOPLE HAVE SEX FOR?

Every person and every relationship is different, and there is no
single answer, though people can be sexually active throughout
their entire lives. (Check to find out what your child means by this.
Is he looking to determine at what age people stop having sex or is
he looking to find out how long intercourse takes?)

9. HOW LONG DOES SEX LAST?

In this case, your child may be asking how long it takes for a person
to ejaculate or reach orgasm. Of course, there is no single answer to
this question—for some couples sex can last for a few minutes, and
for others, much longer. What may be interesting is to explore why
your child is asking. Is it because he has heard about premature

ejaculation, read about performance enhancers, or has certain expectations based upon the media?

10. **WHAT'S SO SPECIAL ABOUT THE NUMBER SIXTY-NINE?**

Sixty-nine refers to a type of sexual behavior. Unless your child suggests or tells you more information about "69," you don't have to specify what the number describes. (Oh, and if you don't remember, sixty-nine refers to simultaneous oral sex between two people.)

Chapter Seven

SEXUAL HEALTH: WHAT YOU NEED TO KNOW NOW

"AIDS isn't a big deal. I heard that Magic Johnson doesn't even have HIV anymore." These words, coming from a fifteen-year-old, pretty much sum up what we contend with today—a country where we have become so complacent about HIV that we are beginning to think that with a few good meds it just . . . disappears. How optimistic and unrealistic we have become. (In case you were wondering, Magic Johnson is still HIV-positive and those meds don't completely eradicate HIV.)

For seven years I talked about HIV/AIDS in my fifth-grade sexuality classes without a single parental objection. Parents—especially those who were sexually active in the '80s, when the epidemic boomed—seemed grateful that schools were committed to talking about AIDS. Last year, however, a mother called me and asked, "Logan, why do you have to talk about AIDS?"

"It's a global epidemic," I answered, "and kids should be aware of it. Besides, children see information about HIV on the news, on billboards, and in television shows. I want to make sure they get accurate information so that HIV will never be an issue for them."

"My children don't watch the news," she responded. Maybe not, but I knew firsthand that her son was highly precocious and had a sexual vocabulary that he was obviously not sharing with his mother.

"Other kids do. Other kids talk. And HIV isn't something that's going away anytime soon."

Her response was so archaic that I almost fell off my couch. "Well, I don't want you talking about gay sex." As nicely as I could, I explained that it wasn't just gay men and hemophiliacs who were being infected. And although HIV is sexually transmitted, there are other modes of transmission that kids *should* be aware of. Before you get all huffy about how your children would never use intravenous drugs, consider the less provocative ways that HIV can be transmitted.

Back before the days of AIDS and safer sex, did you ever take an oath of friendship? My best friend and I did. We pricked our fingers with a needle and joined our eight-year-old blood together, signifying that we were "blood sisters" forever. Or how about diabetic children who give themselves insulin shots every day? Don't we think that they need to know about the risks of sharing needles and exchanging fluids? For these two reasons alone, children need to be informed about HIV. By teaching kids about HIV/AIDS, we are not trying to scare them, we are trying to protect them (and in the case of "blood oaths," to get them to find another, safer ritual). As far as I and many health organizations are concerned, it is never too early to start teaching our children about AIDS.

Thankfully, the majority of parents I have worked with have not complained about HIV/AIDS education. They recognize that it is essential to educate kids about HIV and AIDS in today's world, where there is a rising global epidemic. Currently, young people ages fifteen to twenty-four represent half of all new HIV cases worldwide (Weinstock, et al., 2000), which probably means that we aren't doing *enough* HIV education.

My generation grew up at a time when the entire world learned about AIDS with us. We have never known a time when condoms weren't used during an act of sexual intercourse. What we didn't know, or perhaps didn't want to know, was that unprotected vaginal and anal intercourse weren't the only means of contracting the AIDS virus—and HIV wasn't the only thing that we should have worried about.

How can you possibly explain how big a deal AIDS is to people who weren't old enough to comprehend the devastation of AIDS in the '80s? If you were old enough to live through these times, and/or lost people to AIDS, you know. But today there is another generation who is not familiar with the history written about in *And the Band Played On*. According to UNAIDS and the World Health Organization, there are an estimated 38.6 million people living with HIV/AIDS, half of them women. So when kids ask, "Is it a big deal?" tell them it sure is, but fortunately we have the tools to prevent it; education is at the top of that list of tools.

It is our responsibility to talk to our children about how HIV can and cannot be transmitted. No, you can't get HIV from sharing utensils, saliva, or sweat, or using the same toilet seat. But having unprotected sex and/or sharing needles with an HIV-infected person can put you at risk. And HIV can be transmitted from a woman to her fetus. If you are going to have sex, condoms are highly effective in preventing the spread of HIV, and there are medications available to decrease the chance of a pregnant woman passing HIV on to her baby. Without honest communication about HIV, however, we perpetuate the myths associated with it. We need to talk to our children; we need to make sure that they know how to be safe.

Use props! If you are going to talk to your kids about safer sex methods, show them what you are talking about. It is much easier to explain how condoms work, for example, if your kids can see, smell, touch, and examine them.

GETTING TESTED: WHAT WE SIGN UP FOR WHEN WE DECIDE TO HAVE SEX

The problem is that when we do talk about HIV with our kids, however old they may be, we may stress the risks and emphasize prevention, but we often forget to talk about the importance of being tested. STDs and HIV are a reality in our lives; being tested is an integral part of being sexually active and sexually responsible. Yet that message has definitely been lost in recent years. One in four people with HIV do not tell their partners that they are carrying the virus—not because they are malicious, but because they don't know that they have it (Kaiser, 2004).

I propose that we have our first AIDS test before we are sexually active . . . you know, a practice run. It's something that we're going to have to get used to, so why not? Once being tested is a part of our routine, it is unlikely that we will give it up. In fact, the Centers for Disease Control and Prevention (CDC) is now recommending that everyone between the ages of thirteen and sixty-four have routine HIV tests. For some individuals, this may be a yearly HIV screening. Hopefully this public suggestion will alleviate some of the stigma surrounding testing.

When I had my first AIDS test, I didn't tell my parents. But in hindsight, I wish I had. It would have made the experience easier. Instead, in a panic (stemming from seeing the movie *Kids*), I stayed up all night calling every twenty-four-hour AIDS hotline in New York, trying to find a testing site that would accommodate me the next day. I found a place on West Twelfth Street where they not only had room for me, but had a rush service as well. It wouldn't take me days to get my results, just a mere twenty-four hours.

The following afternoon, during my lunch break from work, I followed a young woman into a small white room. She took out a blue sheet of paper and began to ask me dozens of intimate questions. "Have you had unprotected sex? Do you have anal sex? Do you sleep with prostitutes? Have you slept with someone who has been diagnosed as HIV-positive?" and so on and so on. When the barrage of questions finally ended, she drew my blood and told me that I could come back the following day for my results. I had to come in person, so that I could be counseled accordingly.

I cannot believe that I did that much on my own. To get my results, I took my best friend to the office. (Yes, the friend with whom I took my "blood oath.") I should have been comfortable enough to share this experience with my parents, but at the time I wasn't.

Now, as a parent, I would be devastated if my son didn't come to me, especially if he was doing something as responsible as getting tested.

If you've managed to make it through the '80s and '90s, chances are you've been tested at some point. And if you have ever had a testing experience, tell your children. Don't let them think that they are alone. We have the opportunity to teach by example, and if that means that you and your teen get tested together, get tested together. No harm can come from it. It may seem awkward, but there is no better way to show your unconditional love and support.

> A doctor won't routinely screen for sexually transmitted diseases. You must ask for specific cultures and tests (which, sadly, are often out-of-pocket expenses). Blood tests can only screen for HIV, syphilis, and hepatitis B and C. Also note that there is no widely used and completely accurate test for HPV in males.

A Last Word About Testing

HIV testing can either be anonymous or confidential. In an anonymous HIV test, the tester is not given any way to identify you. This means that there is no way that the results of your HIV test can be provided to a third party (insurance company, employer, and so on). In a confidential HIV test, your personal information is attached to the results. If you give permission for the tester to share any of your medical information with other parties, such as your insurer, your HIV test results will be released as well. Before you take an HIV test, make sure you know what kind of test it is.

HIV ISN'T THE ONLY THING OUT THERE

Unfortunately, there are many sexually transmitted diseases (STDs) in our world and teens are frequently exposed to and contract them. (Often the terms STDs and STIs—sexually transmitted infections—are used interchangeably. However, as the CDC and SIECUS still use STD in their publications, I have chosen to as well.) One in four teens in America contracts a sexually transmitted disease every year (AGI, 1994), and not all of them are curable. (For more information about STDs, see Appendix A.) We need to be more familiar with our bodies, especially our genitals. If something ever seems unusual, smells bad, produces strange discharge, burns, and so on, there may be an infection brewing. The better we know ourselves, the faster we can act if there is a problem. Unfortunately, many sexually transmitted diseases have no symptoms, especially in the early stages of infection. This is why it is imperative that people who are sexually active be protected and tested regularly.

BUT WE CAN PROTECT OURSELVES

The best protection for someone who is going to be sexually active is a condom. Yes, the good ol' condom. It is, without a doubt, the best protection we currently have against both pregnancy and sexually transmitted diseases. While recently there has been an insidious wave of anticondom rhetoric, science has consistently proven condom effectiveness. Even with viral skin-to-skin STDs like HPV and herpes, condoms have been found to decrease the spread of transmission when used consistently and correctly, especially when skin lesions are covered.

Many people talk about condoms, but not everyone knows what one is. And if you haven't seen them in a while, you might need a refresher. A condom is a sheath that is rolled down a man's erect penis. When a man ejaculates, semen is caught in the condom's tip so that fluid does not make direct contact with a partner's body. Condoms are for single use only—for every new sexual act a new condom must be used.

If you have ever wandered down the aisles of your drugstore you have seen a range of condoms and condom accessories; it can be an overwhelming experience. The majority of condoms on the market are made out of latex, but companies do sell versions made out of polyurethane for people with latex allergies. Lambskin condoms are still produced, but these are only effective against preventing pregnancy. They do not offer good protection against STDs because of the porous nature of lambskin. Many condoms are lubricated, some with spermicide, others with a more natural water-based lubricant. (Water-based lubes must be used with latex condoms because oils will erode the latex and render them less effective.) Note that spermicide is not a necessity. It doesn't protect against STDs, only pregnancy, and multiple spermicide use per day may irritate the vagina and anus and cause abrasions, which can actually increase infections. There are many condoms on the market that are not produced with spermicidal lubricant.

Do not fall for the misinformation about condoms spread by certain religious or political factions. Correct and consistent condom use—meaning using a condom for every sexual encounter—has been shown to be highly effective protection against pregnancy, HIV/AIDS, gonorrhea, chlamydia, herpes, and HPV. Unfortunately, with the prevalence of abstinence-only education programs, factual information about condoms has been removed from some public forums. Even the condom fact sheet on the CDC Web site is more difficult to read and understand. In 2002, the Bush administration removed scientific fact-based information about condoms from the site and revised it so that the material wouldn't contradict abstinence-only ideology. What remains is a confusing document that doesn't elucidate proper condom usage and effectiveness. It is our responsibility to assure our children that if and when they decide to be sexually active, condoms are *crucial* to maintaining their sexual health. Research has shown that talking to children about condom use has great benefits for their future sexual health. Teenagers whose parents speak to them about the importance of condoms are twenty times more likely to use condoms regularly and three times more likely to use a condom "the first time" (Miller, et al., 1998). And the use of a condom the first time does make a difference, as it builds the foundation for future regular condom use (Shafii, et al., 2004). There has never been a better time to start talking to your children and teenagers about how they should protect themselves, whether they are sexually active now or in the future.

If you haven't been a teenager recently or haven't had to use condoms or other methods of birth control, you may be a little out of touch with the world of contraception. (Of course, if you are out there in the dating world again, you are going to need this information as much as your children do.) Contraceptive technology changes all the time, which is why it is so difficult to keep up with what's new and what's effective. Appendix B provides an overview of the most commonly used contraceptive methods and tips on how to use them.

SO YOU KNOW WHAT A CONDOM IS . . . BUT WILL YOU SHOW YOUR KIDS HOW TO USE IT?

My parents were big supporters of the local AIDS center and hospital in my community. My mom even served as chairperson of the AIDS Awareness Committee at the hospital. One night, after my parents had come home from a parent training session at the hospital, they told my sister and me that we would be doing a safer-sex activity after dinner the next night. I couldn't imagine what it was and was even more shocked when my mother whipped out a banana and a condom after we finished our chicken breasts. "What are you doing?" I asked her.

"I want you to know how to put on a condom . . . when the time is right."

Although I was initially horrified by the thought of having to do this with one of my parents watching over me, I knew I had no choice. So there I was, rolling a condom down the shaft of the banana, pinching the tip so that there were no air bubbles, and feeling generally mortified. But I'm glad I did it.

If you have no idea how to use a condom (or anything else, for that matter) have no fear. You are surely not alone. Thankfully, these are skills that anyone can develop. All it takes is a little time and practice. And you know what? There is no harm in whipping out another banana and practicing by yourself so that when you do show your child, you can do it perfectly. Yes, Appendix B has how-to instructions.

CONDOMS: NOT JUST FOR INTERCOURSE ANYMORE

I know, you're probably thinking, "Yeah, sure—wear condoms for oral sex?" Your teens are thinking the same thing. But infections can spread through oral sex. There are condoms designed specifically for oral sex that come in a range of flavors. My classes invariably find this very funny, but if someone is going to perform a blow job, or receive one, this is the time to whip out that Mint Tingle. (Remember: Condoms with spermicide should not be used for oral sex. The taste is terrible and it will numb your tongue.)

A few years ago, in an effort to begin a dialogue about safe oral sex, I asked eleventh-grade students if they or "people they knew" had unprotected intercourse. They responded no. "What about oral sex? Do you or anyone you know have unprotected oral sex?" The looks on their faces were priceless. They laughed. "Yeah, of course. What else would we do?" I replied, "You could use a condom." They looked at me with shock and horror. One boy said, "What's the point?" while his classmates nodded in agreement.

The men and women who became sexually active in the late '70s, when the only thing to worry about was getting pregnant (anything else could be cured with penicillin), faced a similar challenge. Why on earth would they start using condoms for intercourse? It was a conversation that took lots of repetition and patience. I explained to the students that they were (in fact, we all were) facing a new challenge. They were responsible for practicing safer oral sex—not just in light of HIV, but because of so many other sexually transmitted diseases. But I could have been talking about algebra or calculus, because they stared back at me blankly.

And then a voice came from the corner of the room. "If my girl-friend ever told me to use a condom while she was giving me a blow job, I would tell her to get the fuck [his word, not mine] out of my house." I waited for someone, anyone, to respond. I could have waited all day, because no one—male or female—said a word. At this point I was close to losing my cool. "Attitudes like that help to spread sexually transmitted diseases and sexual ine-quality. We need to start demanding protection from all of our partners. And if they refuse, then they don't get sex. There's no room for negotiation."

I hope your teen never gets involved with someone so obviously selfish and ignorant. You can help by teaching them that sex, in-cluding oral sex, should be both pleasurable and safe. We all need to be protected—and we and our partners need to be tested, regularly.

The Elusive Dental Dam

It would be remiss of me not to mention that couples can also be pro-tected when a woman is the recipient of oral sex. The difference is that finding the right protection may take a little more forethought be-cause dental dams are not as popular as condoms. Dental dams are latex barriers that are placed (and held) over a woman's vulva so that the mouth doesn't make direct contact with the genitals. Unfortu-nately, dental dams are not as widely available as condoms, so there are times when you have to make your own. Saran Wrap will work (nonmicrowaveable, please—the one for the microwave is porous), or you can make one out of a condom (see pages 129 and 222).

There are some STDs (herpes and certain strains of HPV) that can spread via *skin-to-skin* contact with an infected person, even when there's no visible outbreak. Always use condoms! They do not eliminate the risk entirely, but consistent and correct condom use has been associated with a reduction of transmission (Winer, Hughes & Feng, 2006).

WHAT IF MY CHILD HAS AN STD . . . OR HIV?

With three million teens contracting an STD each year (AGI, 1994), it is quite possible that one of your teens knows he has one, has one without knowing it, or knows someone who does. And if you're like most parents, you probably don't know about it or if he has told his partners. A mother once wrote me that her teenage son was HIV-positive and she wasn't sure if he had told his girlfriend. She wondered if it was her responsibility to notify her. I believe that parents need to talk to their teens about the importance of revealing their status to people they are sleeping with. You can threaten to tell their partners, but first strongly encourage them to be truthful. If your child says, "Yeah, I told her," then the three of you should be able to have a conversation about it together. (That should get him to talk.) We need to empower our children to take care of sexual communication on their own. Being sexually active comes with responsibilities . . . this is simply another one of them. (Whether it is HIV or any sexually transmitted disease, the advice remains the same, but be aware that with HIV there may be legal implications as well. And make sure your teen knows it.)

But what if your teen is on the receiving end of this conversation and it is his partner who is HIV-positive? Freaking out probably isn't going to do much good; your teen will be dealing with his own anxiety regarding his partner's disclosure. It is your job to talk him through this calmly and rationally. (I know, I know, it's almost impossible to be calm in this position, but try your best!) There are some things to keep in mind: Your teen's partner cared enough about him to be honest about her status. That should be commended, because "coming out" (with your sexual health status or your sexual orientation) is not an easy thing to do.

When you sit down with your teen, remember that this isn't a decision to make hastily. Tell your teen that it's okay to take some time to think about this news; there is no script for how to handle this and they don't have to make any immediate decisions. But you are a parent—and you can be honest with them, too. Explain that this news is scary for you as well, but no matter what he chooses, you want him to stay safe and healthy. If you feel comfortable, ask your teen if both of you can speak to his partner (and maybe the parents) about this together. Maybe her response will put you at ease. But you need to know your facts if you are going to engage in a conversation about HIV. There are very clear means of transmission; you should understand them.

Teens sometimes forget that in order for these methods to work, they must be used correctly and consistently. Talk to them about what this means and how to achieve this.

SHOW-AND-TELL IS NOT JUST FOR CHILDREN

Whenever I teach classes about contraception, I always try to bring in some of the supplies I am talking about (depending upon the politics of the school, of course). It's really easy to talk about condoms, diaphragms, and birth control pills in the abstract, but how can we effectively educate without showing our children what exactly we are talking about? When I pass out condoms, everyone is excited to see them, feel them, and figure out what all the hype is about. Considering the media rarely show characters engaging in safer sex, condoms are part of our vocabulary, but only in theory.

When you decide to teach your kids about contraception and safer sex, make sure that you show them a condom. (If you don't have condoms, buy some.) If you are on the pill, show them what your pill pack actually looks like; if a diaphragm, show them the diaphragm. Try not to assume that your child—or your teen, for that matter—knows what on earth you are talking about when you throw around these terms.

It is important for parents to explain what contraception means, and that contraceptive methods have one goal: to prevent a woman from becoming pregnant. Many children don't understand the distinction between preventing pregnancy and protecting against STDs.

Though the number of choices may be confusing, contraceptive options are often categorized by how they work. For example, do they act as a barrier? Do they contain hormones? Do they require

> There is no surefire safer-sex option that will eliminate the risk of STDs completely. The combination of condoms, honest communication between partners, and regular STD/HIV testing offers the best protection. The earlier we explain this to our children, the more confident we can be that our children will know how to be (and will be) sexually healthy.

surgical intervention? Barrier methods are those that block semen from entering the cervix. Diaphragms, condoms, cervical caps, and contraceptive sponges are examples of barrier contraceptives. Hormonal methods (for example, birth control pills, the patch, Implanon, and NuvaRing) are made from the female sex hormones and manipulate a woman's menstrual cycle to prevent conception and implantation. IUDs are devices that a doctor inserts into a woman's uterus to prevent fertilization and implantation, and surgical methods include tubal ligation and vasectomies, far more permanent methods of birth control.

Aside from condoms and male sterilization (vasectomy), all of the contraceptive methods on the market are either taken or used by women. Even though they may not wear or ingest these other methods, men need to be equally responsible for safer sex. Just because a woman takes birth control pills doesn't mean a man is completely free from responsibility. It isn't a bad idea to suggest that our sons share the financial burden of contraception. Even if they aren't the ones taking it, they are benefiting from its use. But even if money isn't the issue, we should teach our sons to share the responsibilities that come with safer sex.

SEXUAL HEALTH IN THE NEWS

Though sex can seem scary these days, there are exciting new advances in sexual health, including emergency contraception (EC) and the HPV vaccine. An emergency contraceptive called Plan B has spent a great deal of time in the news over the last few years. After a lengthy and heated battle, in August 2006 the FDA endorsed over-the-counter sale of Plan B to women eighteen and older. If you don't have daughters or you didn't follow the Senate debate, you might not even know what on earth this controversial medication is unless I call it by its common name, "the morning-after pill." Ah, you've heard of it. . . .

I dislike the term "morning-after pill" immensely. For me it conjures up an image of a woman with smeared mascara waking up in bed and saying, "Oh, no, what did I do? Oops." For some reason, it sounds misogynistic, or maybe it's just because it makes me think of the Jane Fonda movie *The Morning After.* Nonetheless, if we meet someday and you want to talk about this, could you please call it EC? Because that's what it really is.

Because of the political implications of emergency contraception, not every pharmacy will carry it.* It is important that you and your teen know where to find it in case of emergency. As part of being sexually responsible, your teens should participate in looking for this information with you. For a quick listing, the following Web

---

*Though according to an article in *JAMA* (Davidoff & Trussell, 2006), the predominant mechanism of action for EC is preventing ovulation, making it no more likely to inhibit implantation than oral contraceptives. (This also explains why EC isn't 99 percent effective. If you've ovulated, you get pregnant.)

site will help you search for providers in the United States: http://
ec.princeton.edu/providers/index.html.

If your daughter is younger than eighteen, she would need a
prescription for Plan B. You might want to talk to her and her
doctor about getting a prophylactic prescription, "just in case"—
not to encourage unprotected sex, but to recognize that no one is
100 percent perfect and sometimes teens make poor decisions.
EC is most effective when the first pill is taken within twenty-
four hours of the unprotected incident; if you are running around
looking for a doctor or clinic to write you a prescription, you
could be wasting precious time. You need to decide for yourself,
but it's a thought.

10 Common Questions About Contraception

1. **ARE THERE ANY SIDE EFFECTS FOR BIRTH CONTROL PILLS?**
   With any hormonal method of birth control (pills, patch, Depo,
   NuvaRing, and so on) there may be side effects based on the
   concentration and type of hormone. These include mood swings,
   weight gain or loss, spotting, or a change in complexion. But today,
   many birth control pills contain a small concentration of hormones, so there may be fewer side effects. Because a doctor or
   clinic has to prescribe birth control pills, it is best to check on your
   particular brand with your gynecologist or other medical
   professional.

2. **HOW DOES EMERGENCY CONTRACEPTION WORK?**
   Emergency contraception works by preventing fertilization and
   ovulation (depending on where you are in your menstrual cycle),

and may inhibit implantation (though there is no evidence of that).

3. **IS IT BETTER TO USE TWO CONDOMS DURING SEX RATHER THAN ONE?**

No. The friction from sexual intercourse, vaginal or anal, will tear the condoms. A man should wear only one condom during intercourse. (Parents need to make this very clear to their children; many people jump to the conclusion that two is better than one, but in actuality two can be risky.)

4. **IS IT SAFE TO LUBRICATE A CONDOM WITH VASELINE?**

It is definitely *not* okay to use any type of oil-based lubricant with latex condoms. This includes petroleum jelly, foods, or any lotion whose ingredients include "oil." Oils can break down the latex in condoms and tear them. Oils can also breed bacteria, causing infections. If you are buying lubricants you should look for those that are water-based.

5. **IS THERE A "SAFE" SEXUAL POSITION?**

First, I would ask for more information. "Is there a sexual position that is safe for preventing pregnancy? Preventing STDs? Preventing HIV/AIDS?" Even though the answer is "No" to all of these, it is always important to have the most information possible before you answer a question. No. There is no "safe" sexual position.

6. **WHERE DO PEOPLE BUY CONDOMS?**

Condoms are the easiest contraceptive to buy because they are sold by most retailers. You can find them in drugstores, online, in supermarkets, and most places that carry health products.

7. WHAT DO YOU DO IF YOU ARE ALLERGIC TO LATEX?

There are many people who are allergic to latex. Thankfully, there
are condoms made out of polyurethane that are good for men and
women who can't tolerate latex.

**8. IF YOU ARE ON THE BIRTH CONTROL PILL, CAN YOU STILL
BECOME PREGNANT?**

Used correctly, birth control pills are 99 percent effective in
preventing pregnancy. But it takes a keen sense of responsibility to
use them correctly. If a woman does not take the birth control pill
every day and doesn't follow the instructions from her doctor, she
can become pregnant.

9. DO BIRTH CONTROL PILLS CAUSE CANCER?

With many contraceptive methods, there are benefits and risks.
There has been much debate over the risks posed by the hormones
in oral contraceptives. Some studies have found that the estrogen in
birth control pills increases a woman's risk for breast cancer, but
decreases the risk of ovarian cancer. Other studies do not support
those findings. For these reasons it is important for your prescribing
doctor to know your family's history with cancer. From there, you
and your health care provider can decide the best contraceptive
method for you to use.

10. DO BIRTH CONTROL PILLS PREVENT STDS?

Unfortunately, birth control pills offer no protection against
sexually transmitted diseases. Couples can also use a condom to
decrease their risk of contracting an STD.

10 Common Questions About STDs

1. WHAT IS THE BEST METHOD OF PROTECTION AGAINST STDS?

Aside from abstinence (not having any sexual contact that puts you at risk for STDs and pregnancy), if you are going to be sexually active, condoms are the absolute best protection we have against STDs.

2. IS AIDS STILL AS WIDESPREAD AS IT WAS A DECADE AGO?

Actually the AIDS epidemic has grown exponentially since the early 1990s. The World Health Organization confirms that there were 8 million people living with HIV/AIDS in 1990; in 2005, there are 38.6 million. So yes, it is definitely as widespread, if not more so than it was ten years ago.

3. IS AIDS THE SAME AS HIV?

HIV is the infection, while AIDS is the diagnosis. HIV (human immunodeficiency virus) is the virus that causes AIDS (acquired immunodeficiency syndrome). When a person has HIV, his or her immune system—the biological network that protects and defends against infection—is compromised. The cells that help to heal the body (T4 cells) decrease in number and make it more difficult to stay healthy. When a person's T-cell count falls to a number below two hundred, he is said to have AIDS.

4. IS HERPES CURABLE?

Herpes is a virus, which means that it can be treated (in other words, if you have an outbreak you can take medication so that the outbreak goes away), but it cannot be cured. Once you contract herpes, you will always have herpes.

5. WHAT IS THE MOST COMMON SEXUALLY TRANSMITTED DISEASE?

Currently, chlamydia ("cluh-mid-ee-uh") is the most common STD. Estimates suggest that worldwide there are ninety million new cases each year. Chlamydia is a bacterial infection, which, if treated early, can be cured. Unfortunately, most people don't know they have it; it is called the "silent infection" because 75 percent of infected individuals have no symptoms. If a pregnant woman has chlamydia and does not get treated, she can pass it to her fetus.

6. HOW MANY PARTNERS ARE CONSIDERED A "RISKY" AMOUNT?

"Risk" is about more than the number of partners, it is about the practice of safer sex. It only takes one partner who has been exposed to a sexually transmitted disease or HIV to make your sexual behaviors risky. And there are people who have multiple partners, engage in safer sex, and get tested regularly who never contract an STD. We do know that the more sexual partners you have, however, the greater the chance for you to be exposed to a sexually transmitted disease.

7. IF A FRIEND HAS HIV, CAN WE STILL PLAY TOGETHER?

Of course you can still play together. If playing doesn't involve exchanging fluids, it's perfectly safe. You can still share clothes, use the same utensils, and participate in sports where you sweat. Where you need to be careful is if your friend is bleeding and you go to help him (you should make sure that you have latex gloves). And, of course, you shouldn't be having unprotected sex with your friend either.

8. CAN A WOMAN PASS ON AN STD TO HER FETUS?

Yes. If an STD goes untreated, it is possible that it can be passed to a woman's fetus or to her baby during delivery. If a woman has an outbreak of an STD, her doctor may perform a cesarean section, just to be safe.

9. CAN HAVING A SEXUALLY TRANSMITTED DISEASE CAUSE INFERTILITY?

If an STD goes untreated, it can lead to infertility, especially gonorrhea ("gon-ner-ree-ah") and chlamydia, which will put a woman at risk for developing PID (pelvic inflammatory disease). PID may result in scarring of the fallopian tubes or other reproductive organs, increasing the risk of infertility or ectopic pregnancy (fetus development outside of the uterus). Because there may or may not be symptoms for PID, it is important for people to tell their doctor or gynecologist if they are sexually active, so that they can be tested for STDs and PID.

10. WHERE DO YOU GO TO GET TESTED FOR STDS/HIV IF YOU ARE SCARED?

First, if you are scared, you are not alone. Many people are nervous when they take these tests, and that's okay. But you are being responsible and should feel proud of that. If you are looking for information about where to be tested, you can find many resources at the following Web sites and hotlines:

- www.hivtest.org/
- www.adolescentaids.org/youth/resource_nationwide.html
- www.aids.org/info/testing.html
- American Social Health Association's STI Resource Center Hotline: 1-800-227-8922

Chapter Eight

PREGNANCY

Kids have tons of questions about how a baby comes into the world. And if you find yourself pregnant with another baby, the questions won't end.

I was pregnant while teaching a sixth-grade sexuality program and had made a conscious decision not to share my status with my students until after sixteen weeks—not because I was superstitious, but because I was waiting on the results from my amniocentesis. I thought it would be easier to tell students after I knew that everything was okay. I would like to say that they didn't figure it out until after those weeks were up. But no such luck.

While most adults wouldn't dream of asking the question, one girl raised her hand and asked, "Ms. Levkoff, are you pregnant?"

I did what any pregnant woman early in the game would do in this position. I lied. Okay, I didn't really lie. But I turned the question back to her and said, "Why, do I look pregnant?" I smiled at her (completely blushing and embarrassed), and she said, "Um, forget it."

The following week, I decided to come clean. I knew she was feeling bad for asking and my class was going to figure it out eventually. After some congratulations I got the response I had been waiting for.

"I guess that you've had sex," said one student.

In my case, he was right. But sex isn't the only way to become pregnant these days. Fertility technology has brought in vitro fertilization and artificial insemination into our parent-child communications. If there's one thing children need to know it's that creating a baby (whether it's through intercourse, adoption, in vitro, or artificial insemination) is an act of love. It doesn't matter how it's done—it's love all the same.

When explaining the old birds and the bees we often become so flustered that we spill the entire story instead of saving some of it for later. Parents forget that they can stop to ask their children some questions, too. Ask them if they know how babies are made. See what they know (or think they know) and determine from there what information you have to share with them. Talk to them about the differences between men and women—that males produce sperm and females produce eggs. Ask them if they understand that . . . and slowly continue from there. Speak for a little and then give your child a "checkpoint" to determine whether she understands. If it seems like she is getting confused, or losing interest, stop the conversation there. You can always share more with her later on.

But just be prepared that once you start this talk, you are going to be bombarded with questions. Babies are fascinating for children, especially when they figure out that they emerged from inside of a woman's body. The process is amazing; part of being a good educator includes acknowledging this amazement. There is plenty about pregnancy that is awesome, simply because something as microscopic as sperm and egg can together create the small being that is peppering you with questions at this very moment. Let them know how wonderful birth is; if they are adopted, let them know that bringing a child into a family (by any means) is an incredible experience—no matter how they got there.

I was talking to a fifth-grade class about pregnancy when a boy raised his hand and said, "My friend Billy, his mom gave birth to him on a cheetah." To which I simply replied, "A cheetah? Really?" even though I had absolutely no idea what he was talking about. (In fact, I kept thinking, "Is this a new slang term that I don't know about yet?") A moment later, another boy looked up from his desk and said, "That's not true." (Phew. I didn't think so.) "Billy's mother gave birth to him in a Jaguar." (Yes, the car. Can you believe it?)

THE FETUS GROWS WHERE?

It drives me nuts when parents tell their children that a baby grows in a mommy's tummy. They'll wind up like some of my sixth-grade students who have never heard the word "uterus." Too many kids think a baby develops in the stomach, the same place your food goes. As an eleven-year-old once said quite wisely, "If a baby grew in the stomach it would be digested."

If we are going to talk candidly about the genitals, then we are going to have to be clear about our reproductive system as well. It is part and parcel of the same larger picture—we don't need to hide who we are or what our parts are. Would we ever consider calling our nose something other than a nose? A fetus grows in a uterus, not in a tummy and not in a stomach. My sixth-graders were fascinated to learn that while it looked as if my stomach was growing, it was actually my uterus; in fact, my stomach was actually being squished (a very scientific word) up toward my rib cage. Don't leave your kids thinking that a baby may be sharing a space with the remains of your last meal. A fetus isn't sharing that space—it has a room (or "womb") all its own.

Fine, fine, I will concede that when they are little, it is acceptable for children to go around saying that they grew in their mom's belly. But at some point, that has to end. A child going through puberty should be capable of using real words and comprehending what is really going on.

THE BEAUTY OF PREGNANCY

Until I went back to work after giving birth to my son, I never realized how much kids associate pregnancy with being fat. How did I learn this? The moment I walked into the classroom, a boy said, "Ms. Levkoff, you're not fat anymore!"

Pregnancy is not synonymous with fat, but children seem to equate a swollen uterus with obesity. Seeing as the term "fat" is filled with negative connotations, pregnant women are subject to being seen as unattractive, which as we all know is not true. If we allow children to associate obesity and pregnancy we perpetuate the problem of negative female body image.

YOU DON'T HAVE TO DO IT ALONE

There are wonderful resources for your first (of many) birds and the bees talks and you shouldn't be afraid to use them. If you are talking to younger children, Robie Harris's books *It's Not the Stork!* (ages four to six), *It's So Amazing!* (ages seven to ten), and *It's Perfectly Normal* (ages ten to fourteen) are incredible texts that explain pregnancy and sexuality in age-appropriate ways.

If you are going to use a book to help your discussion, here are a few tips that you may want to keep in mind:

1. Read the book first to see if you are comfortable with the material and presentation.
2. You can always photocopy chapters that you feel are appropriate if you don't want your child to read the entire book at once.
3. Read the book *with* your kids so that you can answer their questions as they come up.
4. Allot time after reading to talk about what they've learned or still have questions about.

> You can explain why women don't get a period while they are pregnant (because the lining of the uterus is being used for the developing pregnancy).

For a little while you'll be able to get away with avoiding the subject of how sperm gets to egg; younger kids are more focused on how cool it is that they were growing inside of their mother. But eventually, they are going to become more curious, and yes, that's where sex comes in.

"Mommy and Daddy love each other very much. Sometimes to show our love, we have sex." Your child may let you stop right there, without even defining sex.

If they do ask, tell them that there are different kinds of sex, but that when it comes to making a baby, Daddy puts his penis in

IF YOUR CHILD WALKS IN ON YOU HAVING SEX . . .

Tell him that you and your partner are sharing some private time together. (If you've told him about sex already, you should breeze right through this.) If he asks why you were making funny noises, you can explain that sometimes when something feels good, people make strange noises. You can leave it at that or ask him specifically what he saw or heard (or what he was concerned about); he may have been afraid that you were being hurt.

Mommy's vagina. Sperm comes out of Daddy's penis, swims up Mommy's vagina, and tries to find the egg. The step-by-step description may sound funny, but its simplicity makes it easy for children to comprehend. You can also emphasize that sex is something that grown-ups do.

There is absolutely no need to keep your children in the dark about sexual intercourse, though using the term "lovemaking" is often too abstract for them. Hey, it's sometimes confusing to me, too. What does making love really mean? We love many people in our lives but we don't want to sleep with all of them, right? Now imagine how confusing that is to children. They love lots of people and may not understand that "making love" is a grown-up activity. (I'm not suggesting that we remove the phrase from our vocabulary; I am just suggesting that for our children's sake, we try to define it better—for example, "Sometimes sex is referred to as 'making love.'")

As children grow, sex quickly changes from something in the abstract to something "gross." Take the following statement from a nine-year-old boy as the perfect example: "I get it. We have sperm,

---

IF YOUR TEEN WALKS IN ON YOU HAVING SEX . . .

She will be completely mortified and will run out of your room as if it never happened. But you can approach her. Tell her, "I know you are embarrassed, but we love each other and are entitled to some private time, too." Set up some rules, like "Knock first."

they have eggs. To get sperm to egg we need to [pause for thought]. Ugh, that's disgusting!"

As your children get older, their concerns and queries will change. Young children are less concerned about sex and more about how families are created. They will want to know what adoption is, why some people have difficulty getting pregnant, and how in the world twins develop. For a while, they will just fast-forward over those sex-related steps in order to get to the ones that they are curious about. And you know what, that's totally fine.

Eventually, their thinking will become more sophisticated and their questions will convey their ability to process what you have been telling them. An example of their capacity to put concepts together is the question that many kids ask: "How do you have safer sex when you are trying to get pregnant?" They have figured out that sex is supposed to be protected, but doing so makes it impossible to conceive. If they are asking this, you are doing a great job.

Technically, there is no way to have protected sex if you are trying to get pregnant (reproductive technology aside). Explain to your children that because you aren't using a condom when you're trying to conceive, you and your partner must be tested and must be honest about your sexual health . . . two things that some teens find difficult to do.

Any time a couple has unprotected sex, there is always a chance of conceiving. Even though ovulation is considered the most "fertile" time in the cycle, it is *possible* to become pregnant *at any point* during your menstrual cycle. This is especially true during puberty, when a girl's body is trying to adjust to hormonal changes and doesn't yet have any sort of regularity.

AND YES, YOU'RE GOING TO HAVE TO TALK ABOUT MISCARRIAGE AND ABORTION

Pregnancy is not always smooth sailing and there may be unforeseen problems. Kids will ask, "What if you don't want to have a baby?" or "I knew someone who was pregnant, and then she wasn't." Young children are not likely to ask you about abortion, but they may well hear of or have a family experience with miscarriage. It is almost impossible for an adult, let alone a child, to comprehend a miscarriage, especially if that particular pregnancy was going to result in a sibling. And yes, children may grieve a miscarriage in their own way. Children become invested in a pregnancy too—they start planning their lives and figuring out what their new, mature role entails. They are going to need help understanding what happened.

Illustrations of a developing fetus, such as those in Robie Harris's books, can not only help a child understand what is happening in a healthy pregnancy but can serve as an aid if something does go wrong. Explain to them that sometimes fetuses don't develop fully, even when we want them to. It's also okay to explain that you are sad, too, but sometimes life isn't fair and we can't control everything in our world.

Yet there are also times when you can control whether you are going to continue with a pregnancy; abortion is an option and you have to figure that the subject will come up, simply because it is a hot-button issue of political and religious debate. When it does, you should be prepared—not just to share your values, but also to provide your children with accurate information about abortion. (And seeing as this isn't something that we all have access to, it's time to get our facts straight.)

Abortion refers to a procedure that terminates a pregnancy. Though our news media have focused on late-trimester abortions (performed in the last three months of pregnancy), almost 90 percent of abortions are provided during the *first* trimester. According to the Centers for Disease Control, almost 60 percent of abortions are provided within the first two months of pregnancy. As a point of reference, at this time a fetus is on average one-half to three-fourths of an inch long. Show your kids what this means; give them an accurate perspective. They may believe that abortion refers to the termination of a full-term baby. And that's simply not true.

Depending on how far along a pregnancy is, a doctor will decide what abortion method to use. The majority of abortions are conducted using medications or by vacuum aspiration. These medications cause the uterus to contract and expel whatever product of pregnancy is in the uterus. Vacuum aspiration, commonly referred to as a surgical abortion, empties the uterus using suction and other medical instruments. The fact is: Legalized abortion is a safe medical procedure, regardless of whether you agree with having one.

Abortion is complicated even for those who don't have religious objections. Every state has different laws about what types of abortion are considered legal, at what point during a pregnancy abortion becomes illegal, and whether a teen needs parental consent to have an abortion. These are laws that you and your teens should be familiar with—in case of emergency, or in case they have a friend who finds herself in a tricky situation. To learn about state laws regarding abortion and parental consent, you can go to www.gutt macher.org/statecenter/spibs/index.html.

PREGNANCY OR STDs? WHAT'S WORSE? DO YOU HAVE TO MAKE THE CHOICE?

Even though the rates of STD transmission in this country are rapidly increasing, there still seems to be more societal concern about virginity, possibly because pregnancy is still perceived as the "worst thing that can happen to a teenage girl." This debate, "pregnancy versus STDs," arose in a seminar I was doing with fifteen-year-olds. Some of them associated virginity with control, and having sex (and getting pregnant) was the ultimate loss of control. They felt oral sex wasn't a serious sex behavior because you couldn't get pregnant from it. There still appears to be a stigma around teen pregnancy, even though most kids will never find out about a peer's pregnancy. In the class I was teaching, a girl challenged her classmates: "How can you say that pregnancy is worse than STDs? At least with pregnancy you have options. With an STD, you don't have a choice. You have it, and sometimes you have it forever." She's right. While I do not belittle the massive responsibility that is pregnancy, it does seem that there are more options available for handling an unintended pregnancy than there are after contracting a sexually transmitted disease. But why do adolescents feel like they have to prioritize them in order to manage their personal risk and the risk that they are willing to take. Instead of suggesting that one consequence is better or worse than the other, we should teach our teens to avoid them both by giving them information and the proper safer-sex tools.

10 Common Questions About Pregnancy

1. IF YOU HAVE SEX WHILE YOU'RE PREGNANT, CAN A MAN'S PENIS HURT THE BABY?

The fetus/baby is protected inside of the uterus. Typically, having sex during pregnancy will not hurt the baby because there is no way for the penis to "hit" the inside of the uterus. If a doctor thinks that a couple shouldn't be having sex during their pregnancy, she will explain why.

2. WHY DO SOME PEOPLE SAY PREGNANCY LASTS NINE MONTHS AND OTHERS SAY FORTY WEEKS?

Since no one can be certain of the exact moment a baby was conceived, in order to estimate when a baby is due, doctors count forty weeks (280 days) from the mother's last menstrual period (LMP). That's nine and a half months, not nine. Seeing as a woman usually doesn't become pregnant until two weeks after her LMP, however, we say that gestation (the amount of time it takes for a fertilized egg to develop into a baby) is nine months.

3. WHY DO SOME PEOPLE HAVE DIFFICULTY GETTING PREGNANT?

In order to conceive, the reproductive systems of both partners must be working well. Sometimes, women have trouble getting pregnant because they don't produce healthy eggs or have problems with their fallopian tubes or uterus. Other times, men have problems getting a woman pregnant because they don't produce healthy sperm. Sexually transmitted diseases can also affect male and female fertility. In some cases, couples have to find alternative ways to have a child.

4. HOW ARE TWINS MADE?

There are two types of twins, identical and fraternal. Sometimes a fertilized egg splits in two, creating two "identical" pregnancies that become identical twins. Identical twins have the same genetic makeup and are always the same gender. In other cases, a woman may release more than one egg that can be fertilized by two different sperm. These two fertilized eggs develop into fraternal twins, who are no more or less alike than any two siblings. (Of course, twins and other multiples can also be "created" by medical technology, too.) Conjoined twins begin the same way identical twins do; however, the fertilized eggs fail to split completely and remain attached.

5. IS THERE ANY CHANCE OF PREGNANCY WHEN HAVING DRY SEX?

Dry sex is the term for rubbing the genitals together in a simulation of intercourse while wearing some sort of clothing, as little as underwear or as much as a complete outfit. Sperm lives in moist, warm environments. If there is no direct contact whatsoever, then there is no risk of pregnancy. But if sperm has any contact with the vagina, there is always a risk of pregnancy.

6. WHAT EXACTLY IS AN ABORTION?

An abortion is a procedure that terminates a developing pregnancy. It may be done surgically or using medication, depending on how far along a pregnancy is.

7. WHY ARE SOME BABIES PUT UP FOR ADOPTION?

Sometimes people become pregnant but aren't capable of raising a baby—they may be too young or don't have the support system or the resources to take care of a baby. In order to make sure that a baby is well cared for and raised properly, some people choose to put their babies up for adoption.

8. **WHAT IS THE DIFFERENCE BETWEEN IN VITRO FERTILIZATION AND ARTIFICIAL INSEMINATION?**

In vitro fertilization (IVF) is the technique of fertilizing an egg in a laboratory and implanting the resulting embryo directly into a woman's uterus. Artificial insemination is a procedure where sperm is inserted far up the vaginal canal (with a catheter and not through sexual intercourse) so it can travel directly into her uterus.

9. **CAN A WOMAN GET PREGNANT IF SHE HAS SEX IN A POOL?**

Unprotected sex in the water is not considered safer sex. If a man ejaculates into a woman's vagina, there is always a chance that she can become pregnant. Having sex in a pool will not prevent against sexually transmitted diseases, either. A couple can use a condom for sex in a pool, as it offers some protection. But condoms were not designed to be worn in a pool, bath, or hot tub, so there is a chance that the chemicals or soaps in the water could affect the latex. But in terms of protection, wearing a condom in a pool is certainly better than not wearing one.

10. **CAN A WOMAN GET PREGNANT AGAIN IF SHE'S ALREADY PREGNANT?**

Many children are convinced that women have twins because they get pregnant while they are already pregnant. But if a woman is pregnant, and her uterus is already housing a developing pregnancy, she cannot conceive again during that pregnancy.

Chapter Nine

TECHNO-SEX: PORNOGRAPHY AND THE MEDIA

A CHILD'S INTRO TO PORN

I saw my first piece of pornography when I was nine. My friend had come across her father's stash of magazines—not *Playboy* or even its raunchier counterpart, *Penthouse*, but hard-core bondage magazines full of leather, whips, and graphic images of sex. I could hardly even blink I was in such a state of shock. I had no idea what I was looking at, nor did I know if these pictures were representations of what sex was really like.

Nowadays a child's first glimpse of pornography is more likely to come on cable TV or the Internet, but whatever the medium, the reaction will be the same: a mixture of aversion and attraction, or disgust and a little (or a lot of) sexual arousal. Even if our initial reaction to pornography is "Ooh, gross," the fact that it's about sex and the fact that it's forbidden invariably makes it interesting, if not downright alluring.

No matter how old your child is, they know something about pornography. Perhaps they have only heard the word. Perhaps they have seen it. Maybe they have acquired their own collection or have it stored away on their computer. Wherever their knowledge base lies, it's out there, and it's our job to help our children make sense of it.

Parents need to treat this subject carefully—if we yell and scream, we only make it more fascinating. If you find a pornographic magazine stashed away under your child's bed, don't jump straight into action. Stop and think for a minute. We need to separate our feelings about pornography from our feelings about our children's sexuality.

It can be very upsetting to come across concrete evidence that your child has any interest in s-e-x. You may feel the urge to berate him or her in an effort to push the idea away. But remember, all children are sexual beings. Their curiosity is completely normal. Even if you despise the thought of pornography, you can't blame them for being interested. Don't make your children feel guilty or ashamed of their curiosity. If you disapprove of pornography, either in general or for them, explain why; but don't tell them they ought to be embarrassed or shame them with misinformed generalizations, like "Only perverts look at pornography!"

The second imperative is to help them to better understand what they are looking at. Children need to learn that these images aren't representative of the "real world." The biggest problem with our kids seeing pornography isn't that it's about sex, but that it's about unrealistic sex. Not every person participates in these particular sexual acts, not every man or woman's body looks that way (whether big-breasted, shaven, with large penises, or surgically enhanced), and safer sex, which is not commonly present in these images, is a necessity. Our children need to separate the fantasy from the reality. It's a lesson to teach with everyday media, too.

I was never caught with a *Playboy* (though I did buy one on a dare at my all-girls summer camp), but I remember being twelve and sneaking glimpses at the Playboy channel when my parents were out for dinner. I used to sit on the floor and flip back and forth between that and something more "appropriate" just in case the cable company monitored how much time was spent on the Playboy channel and could notify my parents. Despite my paranoia I continued to watch—not just out of curiosity, but because even at twelve I experienced strange tingly feelings that I'd later realize was sexual arousal.

Whether you are male, female, young, or old, pornography is fascinating for many reasons. It's also ubiquitous, not only "on demand" but popping up when we least expect it.

It is possible that one day your child will come home from a play-date upset because she saw something pornographic. Though your first response will probably be to panic, take a breath. Ask her how she saw pornography. Was it in the family's DVD player and her friend just happened to press the PLAY button on the remote? Or did her friend deliberately turn it on? Was it in a magazine, and whose? Was it on the computer? Then what Web site, and was it found accidentally or did her friend set out to show it to her? Depending on the answers, you may also want to call her friend's parents and calmly tell them what happened. They may already know about it, or it may come as a surprise. Don't assign blame, just talk.

Also ask your child what exactly is making her upset, so that you can talk her through it. Perhaps it was the nudity, perhaps it was the sound of people moaning and screaming. Have her be specific about what she saw. If our children are talking about pornography we need to determine who (or what) is teaching them about it and deal with it accordingly. That may mean parental controls on the computer and television. Or it may even mean a talk with your older child, if he was the one to introduce his sibling to porn.

PORNOGRAPHY AND OLDER KIDS

One day when I was doing teacher training at an urban middle school, a teacher asked me, "What do the students *not* have to learn about?" I answered the only way I knew how. There is nothing that they shouldn't learn—if students have a question about something, then it is important that they learn about it from us, and not from the numerous unreliable sources ready to teach them.

Sometimes I hand the floor over to my class and ask them what they would like to talk about. Many times, they respond: "Can we talk about pornography?"

It speaks volumes that pornography is at the top of their list—and this isn't strictly coming from boys; these questions come from girls, too. I am happy to talk about pornography, because teens need to learn how to critically view their media, both the tame and the graphic.

I asked a class of thirteen- and fourteen-year-olds to think about what, if anything, they might learn from pornography. (It's often best to let your kids do the brainstorming. If answers come from us, the adults, we are often perceived as lecturing or preaching.) The students came up with a long list of thoughts, including: You can learn how to have sex, you see women with extra-large breasts, you primarily see women "doing things" to guys, and you assume that sex always looks like what you see.

"What about safer sex? Do porn movies show you how to talk to your partners about sex?" (They answered: "No.")

"What about testing? Do you see people getting tested in the movies?" (They answered: "No.")

Last, I asked them, "Do you see people using condoms?" Surprisingly, one boy answered, "Yes." Turns out he thought—since he *knew* no one would ever have unprotected sex—that they were using invisible condoms!

In reality, according to a Kaiser HIV/AIDS Report (2004), only 17 percent of adult film actors use condoms regularly. This is a shocking statistic for adults to fathom, so you can imagine how difficult it is to explain to kids who know that we live in a world with an AIDS epidemic and millions of STD infections. There is no good way to justify why people choose to have condomless sex. (It should be said that the adult film industry is way ahead of us in terms of mandatory STD testing—in fact, we should be following their lead in that respect.)

Not all pornography is bad. In fact, for the majority of adults who are able to separate the fantasy from the reality, pornography has a purpose. It can turn us on and give us outlets to explore our fantasies safely. But for impressionable children, pornography can complicate their already imperfect sexuality education. As parents, we should be able to talk openly about pornography. Even if you are against it in all of its forms, we have to explain our stance to our children, and give them the tools to critically look at what they are exposed to.

Whether it's through pop-up ads on the Internet, cable on demand, late-night Cinemax movies when they are supposed to be asleep, or even the occasional nudie magazine that a friend slips into their backpack, they are exposed to porn.

Our conventional pop culture has gone adult, too. Numerous celebrities have released (or accidentally lost) their own sex tapes in an attempt to garner publicity. Even Screech (yes, the scrawny kid from *Saved by the Bell*) created and sold his own tape in 2006. Pornography is no longer a career killer—for some it can be career-invigorating. This is presumably not what we want our kids to learn. We want them to know that the best relationships need a sphere of privacy, or at least let them know that public displays of sex have consequences.

TEENS, SEX, AND TECHNOLOGY: A COMPLICATED COMBINATION

The combination of digital technology, the Internet, and adolescence poses certain unique problems. Wherever you live, your children are documenting their lives. Sometimes they are taking pictures of friends hanging out, other times they are taking pictures in their locker rooms, and then there may be occasions when they are taking pictures of themselves or others engaged in sexual activities. They aren't worried about you seeing these photos; they don't need you to take them to the store to get them developed. With a click of a button these images, no matter how tame or graphic, can be uploaded where everyone can view them.

While teen sex in all its forms is part of growing up, technology has changed the culture of traditional teen experimentation. Exhibitionism now has real-life implications, as these pictures are often posted on networking sites, including MySpace, Facebook, and Friendster, for all to see.

Colleges and employers have been aggressive about checking people's public profiles to gather as much information about applicants as possible. While someone's sexual orientation or activity should never be used as a pretext for discrimination, it is important to consider what these highly sexed profiles make someone think about you. What kind of person would post suggestive and explicit photos of themselves and their friends for all to see? Put yourself in a college's shoes. Would this be the type of candidate you would be proud to have at your institution? If there is information about you on the Web, someone can (and always will) find it. There is no such thing as anonymity, and teens just can't seem to grasp this. Take a look for yourself. Type your own name into Google or some other search engine and see what comes up. You'll be amazed, and possibly horrified, at what is actually out there. As parents, we have a responsibility to teach our children how to use the Internet and tell them why and how best to use certain sites.

There is no doubt that teens need privacy and are entitled to a modicum of it. But the days of key-locked diaries are gone; journals have gone public and we can access them. (By the way, if your child does happen to keep a traditional diary, don't read it! It's clearly meant to be private. Public online journals are not the same, however, and do not require the same parental code of trust.) These often exaggerated profiles that they build online are begging to be viewed—including by you. There may be no better way of gauging your children's innermost thoughts, their friends, and their activities than viewing their online profiles. This is not snooping: There can be no assumption of privacy on the Internet, and I would suggest you tell your teen quite frankly that you will be looking at their profile or blog from time to time. Nothing on the Internet is private—a lesson better learned at home than at the hands of a vindictive peer.

The Internet has allowed teenagers to become exhibitionists—and in some cases, pornographers themselves. While this is not an indictment of the Internet, there is something to be said for taking a cold, hard look at the medium.

> If your child has a camera phone, set up some rules. Camera phones are not for taking suggestive photos, nor are they for exploiting peers. If you are paying for your child's phone, you are entitled to see their photos.

I have heard of girls who send suggestive or pornographic images of themselves to their crush, only to be devastated when he sends the pictures and/or videos to all of his friends, who in turn send them to all of their friends. A not-so-urban legend tells of a young girl who had to flee her city because her simulated masturbation video made it into the wrong hands. Is it a big surprise that a teen would forward these provocative e-mails around, especially if they were from someone he didn't care about? Teenagers are impulsive, self-centered, and notoriously oblivious to the consequences of their actions. It's our job to steer them in a better direction. I'm not talking just about boys, either. Girls, too, use the Internet to exploit, bully, and humiliate peers. Talk to your kids about what it means to be respectful of themselves and others; make it clear that you expect that they won't take advantage of their partners or situations. Boys and girls both have a lot to learn about integrity and only we can teach them.

MEDIA VERSUS REAL LIFE

It is your responsibility to oversee your children's media consumption. Yes, there, I said it. Repeatedly throwing them in front of a screen to entertain them while you are off in another room is not good parenting, though I will admit that sometimes you can't help it. But even when you can't be there yourself, there are ways to monitor your computer or use the V-chip in your television. Not that you need to rewire your whole house. All it takes is a little time with your kids, paying attention to the programs they're watching and the Web sites they're surfing. If you don't have any idea what they're watching, now is the time to find out. It's never too late to start talking to them about what they watch on a regular basis.

I cannot begin to tell you how many of my nine-year-old students have asked me about something they heard on *Family Guy* (a Fox

Don't forget about MTV, which—if you didn't know—rarely plays music videos anymore. Programs are full of drunken spring breaks, threesomes, documentaries about teen excess, and public service announcements about sexual health. Watch these, too, and you might have something else to talk to your children about.

cartoon chock-full of adult innuendoes). Parents, just because a show is animated doesn't make it appropriate for children. If you are going to let your children watch whatever they like, that's fine, but watch it with them. This way, you can tackle any misinformation or explicit material as it comes up. When one girl kisses another on *America's Next Top Model* or *The Real World* or reruns of *The O.C.*, why not ask your child, "Is this something that happens with your friends?" Just watching a television show may initiate a valuable dialogue. And think about it. It's much easier to use examples from the media when we talk to our teens than to come out and say, "By the way, honey, have you ever hooked up with someone of your own sex?"

Older teens are quick to recognize (and become frustrated with) the media's unrealistic portrayal of sex in relationships. Characters go from a first kiss in one episode to debating whether they should have sex in the next. There is no in-between, no progression of behaviors leading up to the big act. If you have had any type of relationship, you know how to watch this aspect of television romance critically and with a grain of salt. But what about younger teens and children—are they capable of sorting through the information?

Most children do not have the skills to examine their media and frequently take the media's word as gospel, which is really a problem because television rarely represents sexuality accurately. Case in point: I was teaching a class about contraception to a coed class of sixth-graders. I explained that if people are going to engage in sexual behaviors, condoms are the best protection against HIV, STDs, and unwanted pregnancies. A student challenged me. "Condoms don't work. Ross and Rachel used a condom and they got pregnant." I am not sure when *Friends* became an educational show, but I am pretty sure that the producers needed to get Rachel pregnant because it made for a good story line. Too bad for the uneducated or uninformed in the audience who don't know that while yes, a condom can fail, it is very, very rare (and most likely because someone didn't use it correctly).

Take the TV out of the bedroom, especially with younger children. Media helps people shape their values and the world around them, sometimes to their detriment. Avoid the situation altogether. This way whatever they watch is in a public space, where you can see it.

In addition to sending poor messages about protection and health, part of what's sad about movies and television is how they often miss the quirky, awkward moments. Sex is far from perfect—there is laughter, insecurity, odd positioning. . . . If we assume that sex in the media is what real sex is like, we are going to be devastated when our reality doesn't match.

Talk to your kids about fantasy versus reality so that they are not set up for disappointment. It is okay for relationships to be imperfect. We're human, we are not fictional characters—we have hearts and minds and flesh and sometimes wavering self-esteem. But real-life relationships—even with all the imperfections—are so much better.

Advertising poses additional problems. Have you seen condom ads on network television during prime time? Probably not. Have you seen ads for genital herpes and erectile dysfunction medications during prime-time network television? Most definitely, yes. Let's think about this for a minute. We give people information about what happens when they get infected with a sexually transmitted disease, but don't give them information about what they can use to protect themselves from those same infections. Sounds backward to me. Our prime-time entertainment sends mixed messages in content, too. For all the innuendo and raunchiness, relationships tend to be portrayed as combative and troubled; there are rarely any positive messages about sexuality. In the media we are exposed to a great deal of violence and a great deal of sex. The problem is that we see the wrong kind of sex rather than the healthy models of sexuality that allow us to feel good, and not insecure, about who we are.

While I attempted to convince a class of high school sophomores about the need for women to demand protection, one student objected. "That's so typical," she said. "Just like on television, women have to be the nags. Why is it always the girls who have to ask for it?" Wow, no one had ever pointed this out before. What are the ramifications of the media showing women as nags in the sexual health department as well as every other way? Why can't boys and men be portrayed as sexually aware and concerned about their well-being and that of their partners? Is it enough for us to talk openly about this? Or should we be encouraging our teens to write letters and take action in ways that make sense for them?

The media is not all bad . . . it give us thousands of opportunities to talk, challenge, critique, and, of course, be entertained. If we are aware of what's out there, we can be forearmed, which in the end is what we really need.

10 Common Questions About Technology and Sex

1. WHY CAN'T I TAKE PICTURES OF ANYTHING I WANT? IT'S MY CAMERA PHONE!

A camera should be used for documenting moments you are proud of. You should not be taking pictures that exploit or embarrass people, including yourself. For example, you should not be taking photos in the locker rooms, in showers, or of people doing sexual or suggestive things.

2. WHAT IS PHONE SEX?

Phone sex refers to a sexually explicit phone conversation between people. Typically, the people are masturbating and/or fantasizing as they listen and speak.

3. WHAT IS CYBERSEX?

Cybersex (or "virtual sex") refers to people who engage in sending sexually explicit messages to partners over the Internet. Similar to phone sex, these "conversations" are also accompanied by the partners masturbating while they read these messages.

4. DO MOST PEOPLE HAVE THREESOMES?

Threesomes are sexual experiences where three partners are engaging in sexual behaviors together. While some people have had a threesome, it is not something that every person participates in.

5. SHOULD I RESPOND WHEN A FRIEND SENDS ME E-MAILS ABOUT SEX?

Once something is on the Internet, it can be seen by everyone. Even an instant message (IM) dialogue can be printed out for all to see. Never put anything in writing that you would be embarrassed by if it was seen by someone else.

6. IS IT OKAY TO MEET SOMEONE THAT I HAVE BEEN TALKING TO ONLINE?

This is a scary question—especially for parents who have never engaged in online dating, or online anything, for that matter. Even if you forbid your children to do this, it's worth discussing parameters (for their future) on how to safely take a friendship from virtual to actual: (1) If you decide to meet someone who you have met online, remember that the Internet allows people to create another persona, and this person may not be what he appears to be online; (2) Tell us (or another adult you trust) what you plan to do so that we can keep an eye on you from afar; (3) Whenever you decide to meet someone from online, it is important to meet in a public place that *you* are familiar with. And don't go alone. Bring a friend, too; (4) From there, use your best judgment. Don't share anything too personal and don't give out your address or invite someone home with you right away. Treat this like any other new relationship; someone should earn your trust, not expect it because you have been "talking" online.

7. WHY DO PEOPLE GO TO STRIP CLUBS?

It is important to explain the purpose of strip clubs to your children simply because they are both revered and vilified in the media. Some people go to strip clubs for the opportunity to watch a man or woman undress; for others, strip clubs are adult places (you have to be eighteen or twenty-one, depending upon the club and state) where some people hang out with their friends.

8. WHAT IF MY PARENTS SEE MY ONLINE PROFILE?

You have to assume that your profile can (and will) be viewed by everyone, including people you may not want to see it. Never put anything in a profile that will come back to haunt you, including embarrassing photos or too-personal diary entries. If your parents do see your profile, be prepared to talk to them about why you have expressed yourself in such a way. Your parents want to protect you, and when you set up an online profile, they want to make sure that you are being safe.

9. WHAT IS BDSM?

BDSM is an acronym that stands for bondage and discipline, domination and submission, and sadism and masochism. These are terms that describe sexual behaviors or sexual roles that people may explore in their relationships. BDSM involves experimenting with different power and control dynamics. BDSM relationships must be consensual, have specific rules and guidelines for behavior, and may be part of a larger BDSM community.

10. HOW DO I HANDLE SOMEONE WHO IS COMING ON TO ME ONLINE?

If someone is sending unwanted sexual or harassing messages to you when you are online, don't respond. (Unfortunately, this

may actually encourage him to keep writing to you.) Instead, try
to find a way to block that person from contacting you. If that
does not work, talk to a parent or another adult you trust who
can help you to contact your Internet service provider to
intervene.

Chapter Ten

TALKING ABOUT SEX: WHY IT'S SO TOUGH

Most adolescents (and adults, too) underestimate the importance of communication in a sexual relationship. When we cannot talk to our partners about sexual topics, we are put into a complicated situation. If we're not comfortable talking about sex to a potential partner, how can we actually engage in sex with that partner? How can we ask him or her about safer sex? Past partners? STD testing? For these reasons, it is crucial that people learn how to talk to their sexual partners. This is not simply for health concerns. If partners cannot speak to one another, how are they to know if what they are doing feels good or how to do it better? Our entire sexual experience may be affected by how (and if) we communicate.

Talking about sex—aside from being central to a romantic relationship—is also a parental responsibility. You play a tremendous role in how your children learn about the importance of communication. Aside from giving them factual information, your ability to communicate with your children models the importance of ongoing dialogue in a relationship. If we speak up, they will speak up. And that's the foundation for a healthy relationship, sexual or otherwise.

BUILDING THE BEST RELATIONSHIP

We are quick to tell teens when their relationships are less than perfect, but do we actually tell them when their relationships are successful, or what to look for in a partner? This isn't always easy because it forces us to consider our own relationships and the choices we have made in the past. And let's face it, we may not be proud of all those decisions. But it is up to us to try our best to model healthy relationships for our own children.

My parents modeled exactly how two people in a relationship should act; they were also high school sweethearts. The fact that they were able to weather the storms of adolescence, college, and adulthood is awe-inspiring. So awe-inspiring that I assumed that I too would marry my high school love. Though it began as a wonderful love affair, my own relationship was far from perfect. However, I fought hard to convince myself that my relationship could be saved, especially because my parents kept begging me to end it. Being a stubborn teen, I would have done anything to prove my parents wrong. It's great if you happen to be versed in the art of persuasion—fighting, lecturing, and criticizing are only going to push your children further away. But more effective than anything is arming them with information about what a good relationship is all about. This enables and empowers them to take matters into their own hands and to judge for themselves whether their relationship is working.

Relationships are built on many things; love is only one of them. The following is a list of important qualities we sometimes forget to tell our kids about.

Trust: Of course you want your teenager to be involved with someone trustworthy. But what does that mean exactly? Trust extends beyond whether you trust that your partner didn't hook up with someone else at a party. Trust is the confidence that your partner has your best interest in mind, that he or she will protect you, and will not exploit your feelings. Trust also means having separate interests or sets of friends without possessiveness or constant jealousy.

Equality: In any healthy relationship, there is equality. One partner should never have power or control over another. Both partners' opinions and values are considered and there is compromise.

Respect: Mutual respect is about appreciating your partner and your partner's feelings. In a good relationship, both partners are free to be themselves and are valued for their individuality.

We must talk to our teens about consent, too. While we don't want to scare our children, we have to explain what consent means ("agreeing, giving permission"), what examples of nonconsensual sex look like (date rape, sexual assault, sex under the influence, and so on), empower our kids to say "No" if they so choose, and tell them that if they ever find themselves in an uncomfortable situation, they can always talk to us, no matter what.

Communication: If you cannot talk to your partner about your relationship, life, love, your sexual histories, and certainly safer sex, this might not be the right partner for you. And if you are afraid of telling your partner how your feel (for fear of your partner's response), this is not a good sign.

SEX TALK AMONG TEENS

I chuckle when I hear teens whispering about some couple who hooked up the previous weekend. They relish the gossip even if they aren't even sure what really happened. Did they kiss? Did they have intercourse? Was it just a little oral sex between friends? Within an hour, an entire school may know what they think transpired, but chances are, what they think doesn't remotely resemble the truth.

Consider asking your child how they define the following words: "hooking up," "sex," "third base," "virginity," and "abstinence." Teens use these phrases regularly but really have no idea what they mean. Every grade, in every school, has a different definition, ensuring that no one has an accurate sense of what's really going on.

A high school freshman health class asked me, "What is sex, really?" I turned the question back to them. They could not come up with a unanimous answer. For some, sex was about penetration, which meant that anal and vaginal intercourse were sex, but oral sex wasn't. For others, sex had to do with virginity, and virginity with sexual intercourse, so anything else wasn't considered sex.

If you weren't already confused, let me complicate this further.

With my students I like to throw another wrench into these conversations by asking two additional questions (which, by the way, have no right or wrong answer).

"If that's your definition of sex, what is abstinence?"

If sex means penetration, abstinence would be abstaining from anal and vaginal sex, but oral sex would be okay. And technically, that would make abstinence not 100 percent safe. (See where I am going with this?)

"What does it mean to be a virgin?"

If virginity is about vaginal intercourse only, what happens to people who are not heterosexual or just not interested in engaging in vaginal intercourse? Are they virgins forever? One of my students suggested that virginity isn't just about a physical act, that the emotionally charged decision to be sexually active, which would include oral sex, is the actual rite of passage. I must confess that I really liked her response. Think about the virginity of a rape victim. If it is the decision—the conscious consensual decision—to be sexually active that is central to virginity, someone who is assaulted would still be considered a virgin.

I know you are thinking that all of this talk about definitions makes sexuality even more problematic and subjective than before, and you're right. But that's what it's all about. Sex isn't, and never has been, a black-or-white issue. It's a fluid concept that changes from person to person. That's why we need to be very clear about our own definitions and those of the people we partner with. During adolescence it's not just the lofty terms that are confusing, it's the little things as well. For example, remember what the bases were when we were kids? First base was French kissing, second base was touching breasts, third base was touching below the waist, and a home run was sexual intercourse. Oral sex wasn't even in my school's baseball metaphor. Nowadays, the kids I teach call it third base. The sexual spectrum has changed but the language is the same. This makes things pretty cryptic—and parents are rarely privy to the code—which is why we'd better start asking those tough questions.

Adolescent sex talk is also complicated by peer pressure. Teenagers feel intense pressure to be a part of the group and do what the group is doing. The underlying folly is that what teens say about sex is pretty fictional. I love telling students: When it comes to sex, no one tells the truth—it doesn't matter if you're fifteen or fifty-five. People aren't honest about their sex lives, which is why we shouldn't do anything just because we think "everyone's doing it."

Along those same lines, teens gossip for all different reasons, and we know that what they gossip about barely resembles the truth. With that in mind, we should encourage teens to make independent decisions about sex, with the forethought to recognize that people will always talk. They should be secure enough with their choices to know that even if rumors spread, they can hold their heads up high because they made a decision that they can feel proud of—even if no one understands it.

Don't take your kids' statements at face value. If they use a term you don't understand, ask them to define it. And if their friends use it in front of you, ask them, too!

ONE OF THE UGLIEST WORDS IN THE ENGLISH LANGUAGE IS . . .

As you well know, our world is complicated by the use of negative terms, and in some cases the sexual double standard is perpetuated by the use of one term in particular. Specifically, girls' use of the term "slut" to describe other girls. These girls may be friends (as in "What's up, slut?") or enemies (as in "She's such a slut" or "What's up . . . slut?"). You see, it doesn't really matter how you use it, it's ugly and unfair all the same. How is it possible for women to embrace their innate sexuality if a word that demeans it is tossed around without thought? In my classes the debate about the word "slut" often comes up. Boys are quick to say, "If girls call each other sluts, why can't we call them sluts?" They have a point. When girls use "slut" they implicitly give permission for boys to use it as well.

Tom, the father of two teenagers (one son, one daughter), found it frustrating that both of his kids used the word "slut" to describe people in their lives. He wasn't sure he understood what his children were really saying. "Are they saying that she has a lot of sexual partners?" he asked me. I don't think so. "Slut" has become a powerful all-purpose insult that typically has nothing to do with your real-life behaviors, though it strikes at the heart of our innate desires and identity. This common insult challenges the very core of who we are—that which we are trying to empower and demystify. As parents, we can and should challenge the language that our children use. And we should also be empowering our children to speak up and out against those things they don't believe in.

And is there really an adequate male synonym for "slut"? Don't let teens fool you; "pimp" doesn't really cut it. (A group of ninth-grade boys tried to pass off "manwhore" as a suitable replacement, but seeing as the hysterics began as soon as it was said, it was clear that it wasn't a sufficient synonym.)

Would you like your teen referring to someone as a "slut"? Challenge him to find a new term—and while you're at it, ask if there is a male version of "slut" and explore why one does or doesn't exist.

THE SEXUAL "DOUBLE STANDARD"

Since the beginning of time, female sexuality has been a complicated subject, sometimes venerated but more often feared, misunderstood, or mistrusted. Even today, women may be afraid of sharing their needs and sexual curiosity because of what they may be labeled. Who would want to honestly share their sexual histories (part of being sexually responsible) if their answers are going to have negative repercussions? I would like to say that if someone is incapable of accepting your past, then he is not the best partner for you. But many young women lack the self-confidence to combat such judgment.

I asked a class of ninth-grade boys how they would feel if a girl they were interested in carried condoms. At first, the young men said, "I would think that she sleeps around" and "She's a ho."

So I asked, "What would you say if she didn't want to use a condom?"

"Then she would really be a slut."

I challenged the boys to think about the implications of what they had just said. Basically, girls were damned if they do, and damned if they don't. I asked them to think more deeply about what carrying condoms really says about someone. After some prodding, they concluded that a girl who has condoms:

1. doesn't necessarily intend to have sex;
2. cares about protecting herself and her partner;
3. cares about her friends and may carry them so that *they* can be protected;
4. recognizes that in a world where teens are exposed to drugs and alcohol (which obviously cloud people's ability to make smart decisions), it is better to have condoms than to go without; and
5. realizes that boys aren't always responsible.

At a girls' school only a few months later, I decided to ask a class of sixteen-year-olds how *they* would feel about carrying protection. "What's the point?" was the first response. "It's *his* responsibility."

"Is it?" I responded quickly. "Doesn't sex involve two people? He may wear it, but it goes inside of you—that makes it a joint responsibility." By putting responsibility into the hands of our partners, we set up an unequal balance of power. If you are in a relationship, the obligations, financial or otherwise, of contraception should be shared. (This doesn't mean split to the penny, but it does mean that girls can buy condoms and that boys can help pay for birth control pills.)

Would you feel comfortable with your daughter carrying condoms?

Can you consider that condoms make someone responsible, not slutty? I told a group of girls I was working with that they should all have a box of condoms at home. They responded: "What if my parents found them? They would jump to conclusions." Yes, parents probably would. But hopefully parents would give their teen the opportunity to talk to them about the decision she made to own condoms, instead of grounding her for her entire adolescence. I would much rather my son own condoms "in case of emergency" than find himself in a position to be talked out of using them because they weren't readily available. But girls are often faced with the ugly reality that their sexual desires suggest innate promiscuity. And if it weren't enough that teenagers talk about the "slutty" girl, parents quietly reinforce these thoughts at home.

Yes, even the most progressive parent may perpetuate the sexual double standard in very subtle ways. Consider how you might answer the following questions.

- Do you think that girls need more protection than boys?
- Do you tell girls "what boys really want" in an effort to get them to postpone sexual activity?
- Do you joke about killing any boy who touches your daughter?
- Do you encourage your son to date or secretly worry that he isn't experienced enough with girls?
- Do you congratulate your son on his sexual conquests but pity the parents of his partner(s)?

I am not trying to make you feel guilty. I mention this because these seemingly benign beliefs can be interpreted (and misunderstood) by your children and teens. It's not bad to want to protect your daughters; but it is problematic when you try to do so without acknowledging that they too have needs and sexual desires. Yes, everyone is sexual—girls, too. It is often harder for girls to express these sexual feelings, especially if they think that someone is going to call them a whore for having them.

I have spoken with many parents who are concerned about their daughters "getting a reputation." I remember in seventh grade my mom telling me to play "hard to get," probably for the same reason. But sometimes the demands on girls to be reputation-free are too high and they get labeled even if they have *never* kissed a boy. The pressures of having a "reputation" can be intense. An eighth-grade girl once asked me, "Will the reputation you have now carry with you to college?"

It's not as simple as yes or no. It is definitely possible that in certain small communities people will talk—remember that in college the girl who turned out to be my closest friend had heard in high school that I was a lesbian. Is it fair? No, definitely not. Which is why whatever we do sexually should never be at the behest of others but rather because it is something that we want to do, knowing full well that people will always gossip, about everything and nothing at all.

LET'S NOT FORGET ABOUT THE BOYS

This isn't just about girls. Boys are affected by the double standard as well. They get the message that they are supposed to feel intense sexual urges and be the "player." But while most boys are curious about sex, many of them are shy and insecure, too. If they don't seem sufficiently "into" girls, or if they're sensitive instead of tough, they may be teased or chastised.

Ask your kids what they think people expect of them. At an all-boys school, I began with the question: "Do boys and girls receive different messages about sex?" They came to the conclusion that girls are taught to fear boys because they are only after one thing—sex. As clearly as I could, I asked, "*Are* you all predatory? *Should* we be afraid of you?" The boys were furious at the suggestion that they were all sexual miscreants. Is it okay for boys to grow up being seen this way? We perpetuate inaccurate assumptions about gender even though our goal is to protect our children. Though we have the best intentions, we do our kids a disservice in the end. Both boys and girls want to be loved, and at some point want to have sex—though not all of them are ready for it and not all of them will exploit and trick to get it. I want my child to know that sexual readiness is not based on your gender but rather on a myriad of qualifications and feelings. Not all teen boys are ready for sex, and not all teen girls are manipulated into having it. If we give our children the tools to make independent and educated decisions, we don't have to worry about them being pressured by their peers. And if they are feeling pressure, they will always know that they can come to us to help them through those tricky teenage times. Our goal as parents should be to help our girls find their voices and encourage our boys to speak from the heart, rather than through male bravado.

NO VOICE, NO PROTECTION

Unfortunately, when it comes to sex, if we don't give our children the confidence to speak up, we leave them unprepared to cope with the world. A nineteen-year-old e-mailed me that she was a virgin (yes, a nineteen-year-old virgin—they do exist), and had finally decided to have sex with her boyfriend. He'd had many previous partners, which wasn't what bothered her. What she was concerned about was that he was refusing to use condoms and she was considering giving in. She wrote, "I don't want him to leave me for another girl, but I don't know if I should push the issue. He just won't talk about it."

Here was a girl who, on the one hand, had postponed sex until she was ready (which is commendable), but on the other hand was wavering in the face of a mate who refused to use condoms. I fear that this is not an isolated story. Many young women (and sometimes men, too) find themselves faced with the unfair choice to either have unprotected sex or lose their partner. The choice for me as an educator and parent is quite clear—lose the partner, keep the condoms—but that's easy for me to say. Teens' early sexual experiences elicit powerful feelings; it's not hard to second-guess yourself when pressured by a partner who seems to bring this sexuality out of you. What kind of jerk wouldn't use condoms? Well, there are a lot of them out there. So our job is to empower our children into standing up for what they want and not compromising their sexual health. We should teach them to stop "asking" for protection and start "demanding" it.

This story can be a great conversation starter in your own home. Ask your kids what they would do if they found themselves in a similar situation. It is less threatening, because you are talking about a third party, not about their own lives. It's a hypothetical situation that provides you with an opportunity to build their confidence and get the safer-sex message across, loud and clear.

> When you talk to your kids about the need to talk to partners about STD testing and sexual health, tell them how you approached these subjects personally. If you didn't have to, explain why and how times have changed. It will give them more insight into your life and your concern for their overall health.

ASKING THE HARD QUESTIONS

Being sexually active means being comfortable asking the tough questions. Do you remember how difficult it was for you to ask your partners about their sexual histories or to take an AIDS test? Do you remember how they responded when you shared your past with them? Or maybe you never even had to ask these questions, if you grew up before these queries became so central to being a sexually active person. Either way, you can appreciate how hard it will be for your children, and that they could use your help.

My own experience was comical, if not pathetic. Shortly after meeting the man who would become my husband, I blurted out, "I am going to take an AIDS test and I think you should, too," over dinner one night. It may not have been the most tactful way of asking, but I was so anxious that it was the best I could do. At least I got my point across.

Informing a partner that you have a sexually transmitted disease is a whole other story. It takes a responsible and courageous person to disclose to a partner that he has contracted an STD. But in a world where 65 million people have an incurable STD (Cates, 1999), we have to be forthcoming and we're just going to have to get used to it. Telling someone that you have been infected is difficult, and it is just as difficult for the other partner to hear. Mike, twenty, was processing the news of his girlfriend's sexual health status when he wrote to me:

> I have a new girlfriend who has informed me that she has HSV2-herpes.
> I am very happy that she has been up front and open about it. I know
> it was extremely difficult for her to tell me. She has given me the option
> of ending the relationship, but I care about her. Obviously, I have
> concerns. I just don't know whether I should have sex with her or
> not . . . and I really want to.

Here was a great example of how to handle the news. In light of his girlfriend's admission, he was seeking out information in an effort to make it work. He wasn't going to end it with her, though it would have been the easy thing to do. A person has every right to end a relationship if he doesn't think that he can handle it. We should give ourselves time to consider the information, however, and see how or if the relationship can progress before we make a rash judgment.

Teens need to know that whether they are on the receiving or admitting end of this conversation, there is no script—no right or wrong response. The news can be scary and confusing, but one thing is certain: We don't want our children to chastise someone who comes forward with this information. After all, don't we want people to be honest about their sexual health so that everyone can be better protected and make informed decisions about safer sex? Talking about your sexual health can be agonizing, but it is a responsibility that we all have. If we have an STD, it is also our responsibility to be knowledgeable about our particular infection so that we can educate our partners and our friends. This means that if we think we may have an STD, we can't stick our heads in the sand and pray that it will miraculously disappear. We need to take charge, see a doctor, and treat whatever we may have.

> Be an active participant in your discussions. If your teen needs to practice what to say to a partner, help them by role-playing the situation.

BUT DO WE PRACTICE WHAT WE PREACH?

Another important aspect of talking about sex is talking to our doctors. In order to be sexually healthy, girls must start seeing a gynecologist as soon as they turn eighteen or become sexually active, whichever comes first. Though nowadays, the American College of Obstetricians and Gynecologists (ACOG) suggests that girls see a gynecologist around the age of thirteen to fifteen, *before* they even become sexually active. But how can we expect teens to open up to their doctors when adults can't seem to do it? Too many of us lie or avoid the conversation altogether.

A thirty-something friend of mine was prescribed and fitted for a diaphragm by her gynecologist. On the day of her next annual appointment, I happened to have lunch with her. She asked me, "Logan, why does my diaphragm bother me when I have sex?" I am sure I looked at her in disbelief. "Didn't you just go to the doctor?" I asked. "She fit your diaphragm—why didn't you ask her?"

She looked me straight in the eye and said, "Ugh, I don't talk to my gynecologist about my sex life."

You may laugh, but I bet quite a few of you light up a cigarette at a bar or a party, then when the doctor asks if you smoke you say no! We should all be forthcoming about our questions, concerns, and sexual health issues. (And this isn't a female thing. Men barely go to the doctor—let alone talk to one.) But if we can't freely speak to our MDs, how can we maintain our health?

Part of being a good parent is encouraging our children to ask questions of people who have access to information, though I recognize that it is not easy to do. Assure your teen that what they discuss with their doctors is confidential and will not be repeated to you. Ideally, if you are able to communicate openly and honestly with your children, they won't need to hide things from you. They will be secure enough in their decisions to talk to you as well as to their doctors about their activities and issues. But if for some reason they cannot do this, isn't it best to know that someone is making sure that our children stay healthy?

10 Common Questions About Communication Kids Want Answers To

1. **HOW DO I ASK MY PARTNER ABOUT THEIR SEXUAL HISTORY?**

   Whenever you ask about someone's sex life, it needs to be done respectfully. Most people, no matter how old they are, are going to want to know your motivation for asking the question. Be transparent with your answer—you want to know about their sexual health status so that you can determine the best way to protect yourselves, together. But seeing as the key to a relationship is reciprocity and communication, it is important to be prepared to talk about your own past as well.

2. **HOW DO I TELL MY PARENTS THAT I AM HAVING SEX?**

   I love the idea that a teen wants to talk to you about their sexual decisions. It is certainly a sign of sexual responsibility that they can share their decisions with you. Now, I am not suggesting that you let your teen and his or her partner have sex in your home (though your rules are your own), but if your children are having sex, I'm sure you would like to be a sounding board for them—someone to come to if they have questions or need help. So what would make this conversation comfortable for you? Granted, you will have a myriad of feelings, but I think that there are some things that your teen could tell you in order to make this conversation more bearable. If a teen is ready to talk to his parents, he should explain to them that he has thought about this decision, knows the ramifications (both positive and potentially negative) of having sex, knows how to protect himself and his partner, and is in a relationship where both partners care deeply for each other.

3. **SHOULD I TELL MY BOYFRIEND THAT I AM ON THE PILL?**

No. There is absolutely no reason for a girl to tell her boyfriend—especially a new boyfriend—that she is on birth control. This is not to encourage dishonesty, but rather to protect the girl from being talked into a situation where she is protected from pregnancy but not diseases. Similarly, I have always told boys (and men) that even if a woman says, "Don't worry, I am on the pill," don't pass on the condom. The fact is, taking birth control pills requires responsibility and diligence. Unless a guy is spending so much time with his girlfriend that he watches her take the pill regularly, he can never know how "perfectly" the pill is being used. And during adolescence, with all the pressures of school, SATs, friendships, and parents, it is possible that a teenage girl may forget to take her pills. Also, we know that people are less likely to use protection when they are under the influence, and there are times when teens get drunk, hook up, don't tell their partners they've been unfaithful, or completely forget that they've been with another person. So to summarize, even if you or your partner is on the pill, it doesn't protect you from STDs. Does a teen really want to take that chance? It's important that they don't think that we are questioning their relationship, but rather supporting it by encouraging both partners to be safe.

4. **HOW DO I ASK A NEW PARTNER TO TAKE AN HIV TEST?**

If your teen asks you this question, commend him for taking the appropriate steps to protect himself. This is a teen who values himself and his safety—and obviously you've done something right! Whether you are a teen or an adult, this is not an easy conversation to have, but it is a necessary one. Point out that this question is being asked not because someone's past is in question, but rather out of care, respect, and a desire for mutual protection. If you make this a shared experience and go to take an HIV test together, it may alleviate some of the pressure. Regardless of how a partner responds, these conversations are important steps in a sexual relationship.

5. **WHAT IS THE BEST WAY TO TELL A PARTNER THAT YOU WANT TO HAVE SEX?**

   Typically we don't jump into bed with someone we have just met, and hopefully this is true during adolescence. If your teen has been in a good relationship, he should honestly communicate his wishes to take the relationship to another level. At the same time, we all need to be prepared for our partners' responses—they may or may not be ready to make the leap. But a good partner should never make you feel bad for bringing this up. If your teen is extremely hesitant about bringing up this subject, it may be a sign that he is not truly ready to have sex.

6. **WHY ARE GIRLS CALLED SLUTS IF THEY LIKE TO BE SEXUAL, BUT BOYS GET PROPS FROM THEIR FRIENDS?**

   There is absolutely no reason for the double standard to exist. If your teenager is asking about this, it presents the perfect opportunity to explore the messages that do exist and fight back against the old stereotypes.

7. **HOW DO YOU TELL SOMEONE THAT HE OR SHE IS PERFORMING ORAL SEX INCORRECTLY?**

   By now I am sure that you are falling out of your chair, or off the bed, or wherever you are reading this. Yes, children—especially teenagers—have lots of questions about performance. They want to know if they are doing something right and how to tell a partner tactfully if they are doing it wrong. Look at the bright side. Someone who is concerned about pleasure—both his and his partner's—isn't going to participate in soulless, meaningless sex. Hopefully they are going to be generous partners who believe in mutual pleasure. But this is not a how-to book, nor is it parents' responsibility to tell their children how to perform sexually. It is a parent's responsibility only to encourage them to talk to their partners about what they need or want.

8. IS THERE A RIGHT OR WRONG WAY TO REACT TO A PARTNER SHARING HIS SEXUAL HISTORY?

Reactions are commonly from the gut, but seeing as how a partner is opening up to you, sometimes our gut reaction isn't the best one to share. Ideally, you should listen to what your partner has to say, ask any questions that you may have, and think about what you've just heard. There is no need to respond right away. It takes time to process information, and you and your partner should be prepared to do a lot of thinking as well as speaking and listening.

9. WHAT DO I DO IF MY PARTNER HAS AN STD?

If your partner has a sexually transmitted disease, talk to him about how it's treated and how you can best be protected. It is also possible to go with him to his doctor or another family-planning clinician to discuss safer sex options. And of course if you've already had sexual contact, you need to be tested, too.

10. WHO CAN YOU TELL IF YOU HAVE AN STD?

If you have an STD, it is important to talk to someone you trust; that may be a parent, a friend, a doctor, and definitely a partner. In a perfect world, people wouldn't respond in a negative way. But just in case, you want to make sure that you have all the information about your diagnosis beforehand so that you can educate the people around you.

SO WHAT DOES ALL OF THIS ACTUALLY MEAN?

Third base may indeed be different today, but the questions and angst that surround sexuality are all too familiar. I have given you a glimpse into the world that our children live in, as well as shared some of my stories in an effort to stir up your own adolescent memories. All of this was done in the hopes of getting you to recognize that though the world has changed, our experiences still have value today. As parents we should feel empowered because it proves how important we are in shaping our children's sense of self and sense of sexuality, which is a natural and innate part of our identity. There is no better way to send your children into the world than to tell them that sexuality is something that they should embrace, protect, and enjoy.

I can't give you the script for talking to your children about sex. It is impossible to create a universal how-to, as every child has different needs and every parent has different experiences, values, and skills. But I hope this book serves as a springboard to furthering sexuality education and communication in your own homes. If I have said it once, I'll say it again and again: Frequent and open communication is essential—and we are all capable of doing it. I know that with a little work, we can all raise the next generation of sexually healthy individuals. Sexuality is too important to our lives—and our overall health—to let the job of teaching our children be taken over by someone else.

Acknowledgments

This book would never have been written without the help of my family and friends. It has been said that it takes a village to raise a child. While that is true, I would like to modify that statement and say, "It takes a village to write a book." I have been fortunate to have wonderful people in my life that have made the writing process a sheer joy. Thank you to my literary agent and friend, Molly Lyons, at Joëlle Delbourgo Associates, for giving me the encouragement and the confidence to tackle this manuscript; my wonderful editor, Tracy Bernstein, and the entire team at New American Library; my attorney, Peter Shukat, for always taking good care of me; my sister, Cameron Levkoff, for being my thesaurus when I had no words and no title; Martha Kempner, Dr. Jane Brown, and Dr. James Allen for reviewing this book in its rough form, and the rest of the members of the Trojan Sexual Health Advisory Council—Dr. Joycelyn Elders, Dr. Eli Coleman, Dr. Cynthia Gomez, Dr. Anita

Nelson, Dr. Drew Pinsky, Dr. Pepper Schwartz, James Wagoner, Phill Wilson, and Deb Arrindell—for their expertise, their support, and for inspiring me to be a better educator; my professor and mentor at the University of Pennsylvania, Dr. Konnie McCaffree, for proving to me that sexuality education is the most rewarding and desperately needed field today; the faculty, administration, counselors, and nurses of schools that I have worked with over the years, including, but certainly not limited to: The Brearley School, The Collegiate School, Columbia Grammar and Preparatory School, The Stephen Gaynor School, Village Community School, Friends Academy, and The Spence School; my students, who constantly reward me with their desire to learn; my in-laws, Drs. Tara and Luis Cortes, for teaching their son (my husband) to be generous, loving, and unafraid to share his life with an outspoken partner; my neighbors and extended family on the third floor who keep me sane and laughing every day; my girls—Lauren, Liz, and Rachel—and all of my friends, whose questions and stories I share with appreciation and love. You know who you are.

Appendix A

SEXUALLY TRANSMITTED DISEASES

In the United States, more than sixty-five million people are currently living with an incurable STD (ASHA; U.S. Centers for Disease Control; Cates, 1999). I thought that would get your attention. The following passages may be dry—it is virtually impossible to describe bacteria with flair—but they are important. Yet discussions about STDs are always tricky, because many are symptomless. The only way to be certain about your sexual health is to be tested regularly, and it doesn't hurt to have your partners regularly tested as well. The majority of the following information comes from the American Social Health Association and the Centers for Disease Control.

BACTERIAL INFECTIONS

In general, a bacterial STD can be cured if treated early enough. If an infection goes untreated (or undiagnosed), you increase the risk of damaging essential reproductive organs, which can affect one's fertility. If you have an STD, it is important to notify all sexual partners so that they can be tested and treated accordingly. While you're being treated, it is important that you and your partner(s) abstain from sex.

Chlamydia

Chlamydia is a common bacterial infection, familiarly called "the silent infection" for its lack of symptoms in 75 percent of women and 50 percent of men. According to the Centers for Disease Control, chlamydia is the most commonly reported bacterial STD in the United States. There were over 929,000 cases in 2004, and those are only the reported cases; there may be many more that are unreported.

A woman who develops symptoms may experience a burning sensation while urinating and abnormal discharge. If the infection spreads, it may damage the cervix and fallopian tubes. It is possible for women to develop a secondary infection, pelvic inflammatory disease (PID), from untreated chlamydia. PID can cause infertility and ectopic (occurring outside of the uterus) pregnancy. Women who contract chlamydia are also more likely to contract HIV if exposed to it. Men with chlamydia may develop some complications, including reproductive damage.

Modes of Transmission: Vaginal, oral, or anal sex with infected partner; from infected mother to fetus.

Treatment: Antibiotics (should be given to all partners). A person must take the entire dosage and course of treatment.

Gonorrhea

Commonly called "the clap," gonorrhea is a sexually transmitted disease that can be spread through contact with the genitals, mouth, or anus. For example, if you touch a gonorrhea-infected penis and then touch your eyes, you can contract a gonorrheal eye infection. While gonorrheal infection rates are on a slight decline, it is still considered a common STD. Over 700,000 people are estimated to contract gonorrhea each year. Like chlamydia, gonorrhea may or may not produce symptoms in women. In men, symptoms can show up thirty days after exposure. Gonorrheal symptoms may include a burning sensation during urination, unusual discharge from the penis and vagina, bleeding, anal itching, or nothing at all.

Modes of Transmission: Vaginal, oral, or anal sex with an infected partner; from infected mother to baby during delivery.

Treatment: Antibiotics and testing and treatment for partners who may have been infected.

Syphilis

Since the popular TV show *Grey's Anatomy* explored a syphilis outbreak, the term (and the disease) haven't been completely foreign to adolescents. There are three stages of syphilis infection, which increase in severity. In its initial stage, the main symptom is a highly contagious sore (called a chancre), which may be found on the genitals, anus, inside the rectum, and occasionally on the mouth. Though the chancre will heal itself, syphilis needs to be treated with antibiotics to be cured. In the absence of treatment, the secondary stage of infection begins, characterized by skin rashes and lesions, and possibly flu-like symptoms. Treatment is essential, as Phase 3 damages the internal organs and neurological systems, and can result in death.

Modes of Transmission: Vaginal, oral, or anal sex; from mother to fetus.

Treatment: Treatment depends on the stage of syphilis infection. Syphilis is highly curable in its early stages by penicillin or, in the case of penicillin allergy, other antibiotics. All sexual partners should be tested and treated as well.

Trichomoniasis

Trich is a type of vaginitis, a common vaginal infection that can be caused by various germs, bacteria, or parasites. Trich, however, is a parasitic sexually transmitted disease that can affect both women (their vaginas) and men (their urethras). Almost 7.5 million people are infected with trich each year and it is highly curable. Symptoms of trich are more commonly present in women. These may include a bad vaginal odor; unusual green, gray, or yellow discharge; burning during urination (or ejaculation for men); and pain during intercourse.

Modes of Transmission: Vaginal intercourse or vulva-to-vulva contact. Other forms of vaginitis (bacterial vaginosis and yeast infections) are not necessarily sexually transmitted.

Treatment: Antibiotics. All sexual partners should be tested and treated as well.

Pelvic Inflammatory Disease (PID)

An infection in the female reproductive system, specifically the fallopian tubes, ovaries, and uterus, is generally referred to as PID. PID is caused by bacteria (commonly bacteria associated with gonorrhea and chlamydia infections) that enter a woman's reproductive tract. Symptoms can include chronic pain, painful intercourse, irregular menstrual cycles, or no symptoms at all. PID can cause scarring in the fallopian tubes, which in turn can cause an ectopic pregnancy (occurring outside of the uterus) or lead to infertility.

Modes of Transmission: Chlamydial and gonorrheal infections, douching (which sends bacteria upward through the reproductive system), or an infection from using an IUD.

Common Treatment: Antibiotics can treat the infection; however, there is no treatment for damage that PID may already have done to the reproductive organs. To prevent reinfection, sexual partners should also be treated.

THE VIRUSES (THE 4 Hs—HIV, HSV, HPV, HEP)

What separates viral STDs from bacterial STDs is that a virus is unresponsive to antibiotics and cannot be cured. If you are infected with a viral STD, you will have it indefinitely.

Human Immunodeficiency Virus (HIV)

If you haven't had HIV/AIDS education since high school (or ever), the basics haven't changed, but hopefully this will help you. HIV is the virus that causes AIDS. HIV attacks our immune system, specifically our helper T4 white blood cells, rendering them unable to effectively fight off infection. Once it infects a host, the virus replicates itself, eventually creating an "army" of HIV cells.

HIV can be contracted when infected fluids with a high concentration of HIV permeate the mucous membranes of an uninfected person. These infected fluids are blood, semen, vaginal fluids, and breast milk. Mucous membranes, in laymen's terms, are permeable tissues that cover certain orifices (for example, inside the vagina, inside the head of the penis, the pink parts of the eyes, the back of the throat, and the inside of the nose).

There is no cure for HIV; however, there are many new medications that decrease the rate of HIV replication. The last stage of HIV infection, AIDS (acquired immuno deficiency syndrome), is characterized by a person developing an opportunistic infection (something that takes advantage of the body's weakened immunity), having a high viral load, and a low (less than two hundred) T4 cell count. People do not die from AIDS; they can die from AIDS-related illnesses and opportunistic infections. While there is no cure for AIDS, there are treatments available that delay the onset of AIDS and keep people healthy for longer periods of time.

Common Modes of Transmission: Exchanging body fluids (blood, semen, vaginal fluids, breast milk) with an infected partner; sharing needles (with someone HIV-positive); unprotected vaginal, anal, or oral sex with an infected partner (though oral sex is the least common means of transmission); an HIV-positive mother to child during pregnancy, birth, or while breast-feeding.

Treatment: Since the advent of drug cocktails and protease inhibitors, people living with HIV have been given a new lease on life. These antiretroviral medications (because HIV is a retrovirus) slow down HIV replication as well as prevent HIV from infecting healthy cells. Again, this is not a cure—this is only a treatment.

Genital Herpes (HSV)

Whether my students are fourteen or forty-four, everyone wants to know, "If I have a cold sore, does that mean I have herpes?" Well, sort of. Both oral and genital herpes are caused by the same virus, so the answer is yes, technically. Herpes is extraordinarily common. According to the American Social Health Association, one in four adults have genital herpes but are unaware of their infection, because symptoms are either nonexistent or mistaken for something else. When symptoms are present, genital herpes may first look like a rash, which later on may become sores or lesions that take a few weeks to heal. What makes herpes highly contagious is that in addition to skin-to-skin transmission, it is possible to spread herpes even if there is no visible outbreak. There are suppressive therapies available for people who have genital herpes, which help to decrease the risk of transmission to a partner. Once you have herpes, however, you will always have herpes.

Modes of Transmission: Vaginal, oral, or anal sex with an infected partner; skin-to-skin contact (when a contagious area touches a mucous membrane or a break in the skin).

Common Treatment: There is no cure for herpes. There are suppressive daily therapies like Valtrex, Zovirax, and Famvir, which treat symptoms and outbreaks. They also help to reduce transmission of herpes from one partner to another.

Human Papilloma Virus (HPV)

HPV is an extremely common and contagious virus that may or may not be spread sexually. There are over one hundred strains of HPV; some are harmless, some produce nongenital warts, and thirty strains are sexually transmitted and cause warts on the genitals that can lead to gynecological cancers. Unlike some other STDs, HPV can be spread through skin-to-skin contact, even if a partner has no visible outbreak. HPV may not have any outward symptoms, though regular Pap smears for women can detect internal cell abnormalities. When HPV produces symptoms, there may be raised or flat white or flesh-colored bumps. Though condom use does not eliminate the risk of contracting HPV, it has been found that consistent and correct condom use can decrease the risk of transmission. According to the American Social Health Association, there are an estimated 5.5 million cases of sexually transmitted HPV each year, or one-third of all STD infections (ASHA). HPV has been a fixture in the news because of a new vaccine, Gardasil, which can prevent four different HPV strains. (These strains account for the majority of genital warts and HPV-related cervical cancers.) Gardasil is recommended for girls between the ages of nine and twenty-six who have not yet become sexually active. Even if a woman in this age group is already sexually active, however, there may still be some benefit from getting the vaccine, even if she has already been exposed to one of the strains. Studies are currently being conducted on the vaccine's efficacy for women older than twenty-six. Since males can be infected with HPV as well, as more research is done some parents may choose to vaccinate their sons, too.

Modes of Transmission: Any kind of sexual contact with an infected person; this is complicated by the fact that many people do not know that they are infected.

Common Treatment: There is no cure for HPV. Depending on the type of outbreak or symptoms that a person has, a doctor may choose one of the following treatment options: cryotherapy (freezing the warts off), cutting off the warts, laser therapy, prescription creams and gels, electrocautery, or injecting acid into the wart. (These options are for HPV-related genital warts.) Depending on the strain of HPV, sometimes the infection will go away on its own.

Hepatitis

Hepatitis is a virus that attacks liver cells and can cause inflammation, scarring, liver failure, and cancer—and can be fatal if untreated. Though there are many strains of the virus (A, B, C, D, E), hepatitis B is the most commonly sexually transmitted strain of hepatitis infection in the United States. Symptoms of hepatitis may include fatigue, flu-like symptoms, jaundice, darkened urine, abdominal pain, and nausea. Hepatitis currently affects over 1.25 million people in the United States.

Modes of Transmission: Mainly vaginal or anal sex with an infected partner. In rare cases hepatitis can be found in the saliva of an infected person, making oral sex an occasional mode of transmission. It is important to note that hepatitis can also be spread through contaminated food and blood.

Common Treatment: Depending on the virus and the severity of infection, there are multiple treatment options (though no cure), including bed rest and prescription medications. Currently, there are vaccines available for hepatitis A and B.

PARASITES

Crabs (Pubic Lice)

I know, let the itching begin. (Why is it that every time you mention the word "lice" your body responds sympathetically?) Crabs are parasites that latch on to your pubic hair (or other coarse hair). Why are they called crabs? Well, in their adult form, they really look like little crabs. Symptoms include itching and visible nits or more adult lice.

Modes of Transmission: Sexual contact with an infected person; although lice need the warmth of a body to survive, there is also a small possibility of contracting crabs from contact with the clothes, towels, or linens of an infected person.

Common Treatment: Anti-lice shampoo.

Appendix B

CONTRACEPTIVE OPTIONS

In an effort to give you the basics, I have provided some brief descriptions of common birth control methods, their pros and cons, and their effectiveness rates. Note that the effectiveness rates listed below are in regard to pregnancy prevention, *not* protection against sexually transmitted diseases. If you have done any kind of informal research about contraceptives yourself, you know that there are two phrases that come up quite frequently: "perfect use" and "typical use." Perfect use refers to the method's effectiveness when used exactly as instructed for every act of intercourse. Typical use refers to contraceptive efficacy as the method is most often used, accounting for inconsistencies and incorrect usage. We should all strive to use—and teach our children to use—these methods perfectly. There is a wealth of information available on contraceptive technology and usage. The following passages should not take the place of a comprehensive exploration, including a discussion with a doctor who knows your—and your child's—medical history. In the back of this book you can find resources for more information about all of these methods, and more.

BARRIER METHODS

Condoms, female condoms, diaphragms, and cervical caps work by preventing sperm from meeting an egg. These barrier methods range in effectiveness, depending on how consistently and correctly they are used.

Male Condoms

Condoms are latex, polyurethane, or lambskin (lambskin is only effective for pregnancy prevention, *not* for preventing STDs) sheaths that cover an erect penis so that semen does not make contact with a partner's body or body fluids. They are the best protection we have against both sexually transmitted diseases and pregnancy. If used consistently and correctly, latex condoms are effective in preventing many STDs, both those that can spread from skin-to-skin contact as well as the bacterial infections. They can be purchased in almost every drugstore, pharmacy, supermarket, or shop that carries health-related products.

HOW TO USE A MALE CONDOM
1. Check the expiration date. Carefully open the wrapper and remove the condom. It will be rolled up.
2. The condom can only be rolled down in one direction. Check the condom to make sure you have it facing in the right direction,

because if you try to unroll it the wrong way, you will have to start over with a new condom.

3. Place the condom at the top of your erect penis. Hold the tip and gently roll the condom down the shaft of the penis, leaving some room at the tip for when you ejaculate. (If you have a foreskin, make sure you pull it back before rolling down the condom.)

4. Gently squeeze the tip of the condom to remove any air pockets.

5. After you ejaculate, hold the condom against the base of the penis while you withdraw. This will ensure that semen doesn't leak out of the condom.

6. When you remove the condom, wrap it up, and throw it into the garbage—not the toilet!

Pros: Condoms are easily accessible. They can be purchased at any major retailer, drugstore, even deli. They have no long-term side effects and do not affect future fertility. Condoms are highly effective (when used correctly and consistently) against pregnancy and STD transmission. It has also been said that using condoms can help a man "last longer" before he ejaculates.

Cons: Condoms are a barrier so there is no skin-to-skin contact; no spontaneous sex.

Stats: Condoms are 98 percent effective when used perfectly and 85 percent effective with typical use.

HOW TO USE A MALE CONDOM FOR ORAL SEX (ON A MALE)

For oral sex on a male, condom use is fairly straightforward. Put on the condom the same way you would for intercourse, but make sure it doesn't contain spermicide. There are flavored condoms made specifically for oral sex. Keep in mind, however, that not all of them should be used for intercourse. If the flavors are made out of sugars, they can breed bacteria in the vagina or anus. It is important to check the instructions in the condom box.

HOW TO MAKE A DENTAL DAM OUT OF A CONDOM

1. Take a flavored male condom and unroll it.
2. Using a scissors, cut the reservoir tip off of the condom.
3. Then, cut across the condom lengthwise (from opening to opening).
4. Spread it open, the flavored side faceup.

Female Condoms

The female condom is a long pouch that is inserted into a woman's vagina, covering the vaginal walls. It hangs outside the vaginal opening and a man inserts his penis into the condom (which acts as a contraceptive sleeve).

I was in college when the female condom was introduced to the market and I have to say, I was overjoyed. Finally there was something that women could use that wasn't hormonal and/or prescribed by doctors. Thus far, male condoms remain more popular than female condoms, maybe because so many women are uncomfortable handling their genitals. Nonetheless, it is definitely another option for couples, especially those who have latex allergies.

HOW TO USE THE FEMALE CONDOM

1. Check the expiration date. Carefully open the wrapper and remove the condom.
2. The condom will have two rings—one at the open end of the condom and another at the closed end. Using your thumb and index finger, squeeze the inner ring at the closed end of the condom and insert the condom inside the vagina.
3. The inner ring will open up and shift into place against your cervix.
4. Use your finger to make sure that the condom is as far up as it can go.
5. When you are ready for intercourse, guide your partner's penis inside of the condom.
6. When you are finished, twist the outer ring of the condom and gently pull it out.
7. Condoms are single-use; wrap it up and discard it (in the garbage, not the toilet).

It is important to practice using the female condom because it can be tricky to insert the first time. But practice makes perfect! Note that you cannot use a male condom and a female condom together as the friction during sex can tear them.

Pros: Women can be responsible for carrying and using their own protection. It is made out of polyurethane so it is good for individuals with latex allergies. Also, the outer ring of the condom may provide external clitoral stimulation.

Cons: It needs to be inserted before intercourse takes place. It hangs outside the vagina and makes "squishing" noises during sex.

It is more expensive than male condoms and not sold everywhere male condoms can be purchased.

Stats: Female condoms are 95 percent effective when used perfectly and 79 percent effective with typical use.

Diaphragm

Though the diaphragm may make you flash back to finding your mother's plastic case while rummaging through her makeup as a child, some women are still using the diaphragm for birth control. It is a reusable shallow rubber cup that you rim with spermicide and insert into the vagina. The cup creates a barrier against the cervix and is kept in place by the vaginal muscles. A gynecologist or clinician must fit a woman for the diaphragm, as every woman's vagina is different. A diaphragm may be inserted up to an hour before sex and cannot be removed until at least six hours after. (Medical practitioners suggest that a woman not leave a diaphragm in for more than twenty-four hours. And if a woman has sex again during this time, she must add more spermicide.) For the most part, couples who choose to use a diaphragm are not worried about transmission of STDs. Their main concern is pregnancy prevention.

Pros: Offers "some" protection against sexually transmitted diseases (not HIV/AIDS) and does not affect your menstrual cycle. It is good for women who cannot take hormone-based contraceptives. You can insert it prior to sex, allowing for slightly more spontaneous sex.

Cons: It may be difficult for a woman to insert and the spermicide may irritate the vagina. It may be costly to have the exam and fill the prescription (though you do not need to purchase anything other than spermicide for the next year). The diaphragm cannot be used if you have latex allergies or have a history of toxic shock syndrome. If you gain weight (ten pounds or more) or become pregnant, you have to be refit for the diaphragm.

Stats: The diaphragm combined with spermicide is 94 percent effective when used perfectly and 84 percent effective with typical use.

HORMONAL METHODS

The following methods fall under the category of "hormonal contraceptives" because they are made from hormones that are found (or made to resemble those found) in a woman's body. These contraceptives manipulate the menstrual cycle into providing constant pregnancy prevention. These methods all require a prescription and pelvic exam.

Birth Control Pills

Wherever I teach, teens seem to view "the pill" as the world's perfect safer-sex option. Unfortunately, it's not perfect. In fact, nothing is. But birth control pills (oral contraceptives) are highly effective in preventing pregnancy when used correctly. BC pills are made from hormones that mimic those in a woman's menstrual cycle. Some pills are combination pills, consisting of estrogen and progestin, and others, like the Mini-Pill, are made from only progestin.

Combination pills work by inhibiting ovulation (the release of an egg) and thickening a woman's cervical mucus; this prevents sperm from getting into the reproductive system. Mini-Pills thicken cervical mucus. Both types of pills also thin the lining of the uterus. Both combination and progestin-only pills come in monthly packs. Depending on your prescription, you will have "active" pills and "inactive," or "reminder," pills. It is important to talk to your doctor about how to correctly use your particular pills.

Taking BC pills requires diligence. The pill must be taken once a day, every day, for as long as you want to maintain pregnancy prevention. The progestin-only pill must be taken within the same three-hour time frame every day. If a woman misses a pill, she must take one as soon as she remembers, even if she takes two the following day. If a woman skips more than two days, she must use backup protection.

Pros: Birth control pills allow for sexual spontaneity. They may help to prevent some gynecological cancers.

Cons: The pill does not protect against sexually transmitted diseases. Hormone-based contraceptives interact with your menstrual cycle. Women who are thirty-five and older, have a history of blood clots, have certain cancers, or smoke should not take the pill. Certain medications may react with birth control pills and decrease their effectiveness. It is important to talk to your doctor before beginning any hormone-based contraceptive.

Stats: Birth control pills are 99 percent effective when use perfectly and 92 percent effective with typical use.

Depo-Provera

Depo, as it is commonly called, is also referred to as "The Shot." It is a three-month dose of the hormone progestin injected into a woman's buttocks or arm muscle. Depo prevents a woman from ovulating—without an egg present, a woman cannot get pregnant—and also inhibits the uterine lining from developing fully, causing a period to be incredibly light or nonexistent (and again, there's no egg to be released).

Pros: Three months without worrying about birth control.

Cons: Depo-Provera offers no protection against sexually transmitted diseases. As it lasts three months, once it is in your system, it cannot come out if you have some type of reaction. There may be side effects during the first year, including spotting, weight gain, and menstrual irregularity.

Stats: Depo is 99.7 percent effective with perfect use and 97 percent effective with typical use. (If you are wondering why there isn't 100 percent effectiveness, the 3 percent failure rate may be due to technician error, incorrect measurement of the dosage, late or forgotten follow-up injections, or a woman may already be pregnant when she takes the shot.)

IUD

The intrauterine device (IUD) is a T-shaped (or as my younger students like to say, "It looks like a pogo stick") piece of plastic placed inside the uterus by a doctor, where it prevents sperm and egg from meeting and implanting in the uterine wall. There are currently two types of IUDs available: Mirena contains the hormone progestin and is effective for five years; ParaGard contains a small amount of copper (no hormones) and is effective for up to twelve years. If a woman is using Mirena, the IUD will also help to thicken cervical mucus. After each period, the woman has to check that the IUD is still in place by inserting a finger (clean, please) inside of the vagina to feel its thread hanging just outside the cervix.

Pros: Spontaneous sex, no pills to take daily, offers immediate protection, and it is long-lasting pregnancy prevention.

Cons: IUDs offer no protection against sexually transmitted diseases, women may experience heavy periods or spotting, and there is a small risk of the IUD being expelled from the uterus, perforating the uterus, and causing a pelvic infection.

Stats: For both types of IUDs the effectiveness rates for both perfect and typical use are over 99 percent.

SURGICAL STERILIZATION

Vasectomy

As discussed in Chapter 3, the vas deferens is responsible for transporting sperm through the male reproductive system. A vasectomy cuts and ties off the vas deferens so that there is no sperm present in a man's ejaculate. No sperm, no possible pregnancy.

Pros: Excellent protection against pregnancy and sex can be spontaneous. Having a vasectomy does not affect a man's ability to have erections or ejaculate.

Cons: Does not offer protection against sexually transmitted diseases and requires minor surgery on the genitals. It is possible to reverse a vasectomy, though there is no guarantee.

Stats: The effectiveness rates for both typical and perfect use are over 99 percent, making it a highly effective method of contraception.

Tubal Ligation

If a woman is looking to control her fertility permanently, she may decide to undergo a tubal ligation (commonly referred to as "having your tubes tied"), a surgical procedure in which the fallopian tubes are cut and tied off so that an egg cannot meet the sperm. This operation is permanent and it is unlikely that it can be reversed. A woman who considers this option must be certain that she does not want any more children. (In rare cases, the tubes may reconnect in later years so that a woman becomes pregnant, or experiences an ectopic pregnancy.)

Pros: Highly effective protection against pregnancy, does not interrupt sex, does not change the hormonal balance in a woman's body.

Cons: Offers no protection against sexually transmitted diseases and requires a medical procedure. While there is a slight possibility that the surgery can be reversed, a woman should consider this to be a permanent option.

Stats: The effectiveness rates for both typical and perfect use are over 99 percent, making it a highly effective method of contraception.

EMERGENCY CONTRACEPTION

Emergency contraception (EC) is made from a high dose of hormones that, if taken within seventy-two hours of unprotected sex, can prevent conception from taking place primarily by preventing ovulation (depending on where you are in your menstrual cycle when you take EC). Technically, EC works just like regular birth control pills, although EC provides a higher concentration of hormones. It is most effective when taken within the first twenty-four hours after sex. It is called "emergency contraception" because it is designed to be used in case of emergency, not as a regular method of birth control. There are a few different types of EC, each using a different combination of hormones. Plan B is made up of levonorgestrel, a hormone commonly found in birth control pills. It does not contain estrogen. Other brands, such as Preven, contain both estrogen and progestin. Typically, EC is made up of two pills taken twelve hours apart; it will not work unless both doses are taken. Again, it is important to note that EC should not be used as an ongoing method of contraception.

Pros: This is a backup method for women when they had unprotected sex, their current form of contraception failed, or they were sexually assaulted and didn't have the choice to use protection. Also, EC does not affect a woman's future fertility.

Cons: EC does not offer any protection against sexually transmitted diseases. In addition, EC will not work if a woman is already pregnant. A woman under the age of eighteen needs a prescription to purchase emergency contraception. Estrogen-based pills are associated with nausea and vomiting (typically an antinausea medication is prescribed with these pills). The more time that passes from the unprotected sexual encounter, the less effective emergency contraception becomes.

Stats: If used correctly, emergency contraceptives are up to 89 percent effective in preventing pregnancy.

WITHDRAWAL

A.k.a "the pull & pray method," withdrawal refers to unprotected sex in which a man withdraws his penis before he ejaculates. Unfortunately, the penis secretes preejaculatory fluid ("precum"), which can on occasion contain sperm and can also carry viruses and bacteria.

Pros: There is no barrier between you and your partner, making for spontaneous sex; it is free and does not require a prescription.

Cons: Ineffective for STD prevention and precum may still contain sperm. A woman must rely on (and trust) her partner to "pull out" before ejaculating and men often cannot "time" when ejaculation is going to occur.

Stats: This method is 96 percent effective with perfect use and 73 percent effective with typical use.

THE RHYTHYM METHOD

Also called natural family planning or fertility awareness, the rhythm method is a contraceptive technique based on abstaining from sex when a woman is fertile. In order to determine this, a woman needs to: have an understanding of her menstrual cycle, check her cervical mucus to determine its consistency, take her basal body temperature, and chart it for a year to identify when she is fertile.

Pros: It doesn't cost anything (except if you choose to buy a basal body thermometer), no barrier, good for people with objections to contraceptives.

Cons: No protection against sexually transmitted diseases; a woman must be diligent in (and committed to) charting her temperature, cervical mucus, and menstrual cycles; it has a higher failure rate than all other contraceptive methods; and you have to abstain from sex during fertile times (or use a backup method).

Stats: The rhythm method is 91–99 percent effective with perfect use and 75 percent effective with typical use.

Appendix C

RESOURCES
Sexuality Resources
for Parents

Advocates for Youth

www.advocatesforyouth.org

American Association of Sexuality Educators, Counselors, and Therapists
(AASECT)

www.aasect.org

American Social Health Association

www.ashastd.org

Alan Guttmacher Institute (AGI)

www.guttmacher.org

Kaiser Family Foundation

www.kff.org

National Campaign to Prevent Teen Pregnancy

www.teenpregnancy.org

Planned Parenthood Federation of America

www.plannedparenthood.org

Talking With Kids

www.talkingwithkids.org

Sexuality and U

www.sexualityandu.ca

Sexuality Information and Education Council of the United States (SIECUS)

www.siecus.org

Sex Information and Education Council of Canada (SIECCAN)

www.sieccan.org

LGBT Resources for Parents and Teens

COLAGE (Equality & Justice for People with Lesbian, Gay, Bisexual and/
   or Transgender Parents)
www.colage.org
Gay, Lesbian and Straight Education Network (GLSEN)
www.glsen.org
Human Rights Campaign (HRC)
www.hrc.org
Intersex Society of North America (ISNA)
www.isna.org
Outproud
www.outproud.org
Parents, Families and Friends of Lesbians and Gays (PFLAG)
www.pflag.org
We Are Family
www.waf.org
YouthResource
www.youthresource.com/

General Info on Sexuality: For Your Teens

Teenwire

www.teenwire.com

Go Ask Alice

www.goaskalice.columbia.edu/

Scarleteen

www.scarleteen.com

Coalition for Positive Sexuality

www.positive.org/Home/index.html

Sex, Etc.

www.sxetc.com

The Sexual Health Network

www.sexualhealth.com

I Wanna Know

www.iwannaknow.org/

It's Your (Sex) Life

www.itsyoursexlife.com

Rape, Abuse & Incest National Network

www.rainn.org

REFERENCES

AGI (2006). "Facts on Sexually Transmitted Infections in the United States." Retrieved on January 14, 2007, from www.guttmacher.org/pubs/fb_sti.html.

AGI (1994). *Sex and America's Teenagers* (New York: Alan Guttmacher Institute).

American Social Health Association (ASHA). "STD/STI Statistics." Retrieved on January 14, 2007, from www.ashastd.org/learn/learn_statistics.cfm.

Bearman, P., & H. Bruckner. "After the Promise: The STD Consequences of Adolescent Virginity Pledges," *Journal of Adolescent Health* 36 (2005), pp. 271–78.

Cates, W. (1999). "Estimates of the Incidence and Prevalence of Sexually Transmitted Diseases in the United States," *Sexually Transmitted Diseases* 26 (Supplement), pp. S2–S7.

Centers for Disease Control and Prevention (November 24, 2006). "Abortion Surveillance—United States, 2003," *Morbidity and Mortality Weekly Report* 55 (SS11), pp. 1–32.

Dailard, C. (December 2003). "Understanding 'Abstinence': Implications for Individuals, Programs, and Policies," *The Guttmacher Report on Public Policy* 6, pp. 4–6.

Davidoff, F. & Trussell, J. (2006). "Plan B and the Politics of Doubt," *Journal of the American Medical Association* 296, pp. 1775–78.

DePaola, T. (1979). *Oliver Button Is a Sissy* (Orlando, Fla.: Voyager Books).

Finer, L. (2007). "Trends in Premarital Sex in the United States, 1954–2003," *Public Health Reports* 122, pp. 73–122.

Giles, G., G. Severi & E. English (2003). "Sexual Factors and Prostate Cancer," *BJU International* 92, pp. 211–16.

Harris, R. (2006). *It's Not the Stork! A Book about Girls, Boys, Babies, Bodies, Families and Friends* (Cambridge, Mass.: Candlewick Press).

Harris, R. (1999). *It's So Amazing! A Book about Eggs, Sperm, Birth, Babies, and Families* (Cambridge, Mass.: Candlewick Press).

Hoff, T. (2003). *National Survey of Adolescents and Young Adults: Sexual Health Knowledge, Attitudes, and Experiences* (Menlo Park, Calif.: KFF).

Kaiser Family Foundation (2006). "HIV/AIDS Policy Fact Sheet: The Global HIV Epidemic." Retrieved on January 14, 2007, from www.kff.org/hivaids/upload/3030-07.pdf.

Kaiser Family Foundation (2004). *Survey of Americans on HIV/AIDS* (Menlo Park, Calif.: KFF).

Kaiser Family Foundation (April 24, 2004). "Daily HIV/AIDS Report: Public Health & Education Group Says HIV 'Outbreak' Contained Among Adult Film Actors; L.A. Health Officials Obtain Workers' Medical Records" (Menlo Park, Calif.: KFF).

Kinsey, A., et al. (1953/1998). *Sexual Behavior in the Human Female* (Philadelphia: W. B. Saunders; Bloomington, Ind.: Indiana University Press).

Kinsey, A., et al. (1948/1998). *Sexual Behavior in the Human Male* (Philadelphia: W. B. Saunders; Bloomington, Ind.: Indiana University Press).

Kirby, D. (2000). "What Does the Research Say About Sexuality Education?" *Educational Leadership*, pp. 72–76.

Leitzmann, M., E. Platz, M. Stampfer, W. Willett, & E. Giovannucci (2004). "Ejaculation Frequency and Subsequent Risk of Prostate Cancer," *Journal of the American Medical Association* 291, pp. 1578–86.

Levkoff, L. (October 2006). "Ask the Sexpert," *Poz* (New York: Smart and Strong Publishing).

Miller, K., M. Levin, D. Whitaker, X. Xu (1998). "Patterns of Condom Use Among Adolescents: The Impact of Mother-Adolescent Communication," *American Journal of Public Health* 88, pp. 1542–44.

Santelli, J., M. Ott, M. Lyon, J. Rogers, D. Summers & R. Schleifer (2006). "Abstinence and Abstinence-Only Education: A Review of U.S. Policies and Programs," *Journal of Adolescent Health* 38, pp. 83–87.

Satcher, D. (2001). "The Surgeon General's Call to Action to Promote Sexual Health and Responsible Sexual Behavior." Retrieved on February 9, 2007, from www.ncbi.nlm.nih.gov/books/bv.fcgi?rid=hstat5.chapter.321.

SIECUS Public Policy Office (2006). "Special Report: It Gets Worse: A Revamped Federal Abstinence-Only Program Goes Extreme." Retrieved on November 10, 2006, from www.siecus.org/policy/Revamped_Abstinence-Only_Goes_Extreme.pdf.

Shafii, T., K. Stovel, R. Davis, & K. Holmes (2004). "Is Condom Use Habit Forming?: Condom Use at Sexual Debut and Subsequent Condom Use," *Sexually Transmitted Diseases* 31, pp. 366–72.

Shilts, R. (1988). *And the Band Played On: Politics, People, and the AIDS Epidemic* (New York: Stonewall Inn Editions).

Trussell, J. (2004). "Contraceptive Efficacy," in Hatcher, R.A., J. Trussell, F. Stewart, A. Nelson, W. Cates, F. Guest, D. Kowal, *Contraceptive Technology: Eighteenth Revised Edition* (New York: Ardent Media).

UNAIDS (2004). 2004 report on the global AIDS epidemic.

Waxman, H. (2004). "The Content of Federally Funded Abstinence Only Education Programs." Retrieved on February 10, 2007, from http://oversight.house.gov/Documents/20041201102153-50247.pdf.

Weinstock, H., S. Berman & W. Cates (2000). "Sexually Transmitted Diseases among American Youth: Incidence and Prevalence Estimates," *Perspectives on Sexual and Reproductive Health* 36, pp. 6–10.

Winer, R., J. Hughes, & Q. Feng (2006). "Condom Use and the Risk of Genital Human Papilloma Virus Infection in Young Women," *New England Journal of Medicine* 354, pp. 2645–54.

Photo by Tess Steinkolk

Logan Levkoff has been a sexuality educator for more than ten years. She lectures around the country and designs and implements sexuality programs for students of all ages. Logan is also a frequent contributor to print, Web, and television media. She is committed to perpetuating positive messages about sexuality and encouraging parents to engage their children in honest conversations about sex. Visit her Web site at www.loganlevkoff.com.